THE AMERICAN KENNEL CLUB'S
Meet the
Rottweiler™

AKC's Meet the Breeds Series

I-5
EST. 2013
·PRESS·
i-5 Publishing, LLC™

The Responsible
Dog Owner's
Handbook

AN OFFICIAL PUBLICATION OF ⬤ AKC FOUNDED 1884 THE AMERICAN KENNEL CLUB

AMERICAN
KENNEL CLUB®

Brought to you by the American Kennel Club and the American Rottweiler Club

i-5 PUBLISHING, LLC™
Chief Executive Officer: Mark Harris
Chief Financial Officer: Nicole Fabian
Vice President, Chief Content Officer: June Kikuchi
General Manager, i5 Press: Christopher Reggio
Editorial Director, i5 Press: Andrew DePrisco
Art Director, i5 Press: Mary Ann Kahn
Digital General Manager: Melissa Kauffman
Production Director: Laurie Panaggio
Production Manager: Jessica Jaensch
Marketing Director: Lisa MacDonald

Photography: American Kennel Club, 119; Degtyaryov Andrey/Shutterstock, 1, 18, 80–81; BLDUMMY/Flickr, 4, 110–111; Brenda Carson/Shutterstock, 85; Mario Castro/Flickr, 67; caspermoller/Flickr, 104; Caylor Photography/Flickr, 72 (bottom); Stephen Coburn/Shutterstock, 31; cpphotoimages/Shutterstock, 46; Linn Currie/Shutterstock, 30; cynoclub/Shutterstock, 4, 10, 12, 26, 27, 28–29, 34, 59, 68, 79, 82, 89, 90–91, 93, 102, 109, 114, 116, 117, 118; dezi/Shutterstock, 4, 57, 60–61, 70–71, 76; Dreamy Girl/Shutterstock, 36; Ersler Dmitry/Shutterstock, 13, 75; Eschipul Rottie/Flickr, 112; Tom Feist/Shutterstock, 121; Isabelle Francais/i5 Publications, 63; Tami Freed/Shutterstock, 100–101; GoDog Photo/Shutterstock, 105; Denise Grimm, 72 (top); hempuli/Shutterstock, 4, 6–7; Ammit Jack/Shutterstock, 16–17, 20, 69, 77, 84, 106; Rita Kochmarjova/Shutterstock, 9; Lilya Kulianionak/Shutterstock, 37; Erik Lam/Shutterstock, 48, 66, 124; Erik Mandre/Shutterstock, 98; Tatiana Makotra/Shutterstock, 25, 58; MotoWebMistress/Flickr, 40, 95; mooney/Flickr, 78; otsphoto/Flickr, 83, 87, 97; pixshots/Shutterstock, 53; Anastasija Popova/Shutterstock, 52; Paul Rich Studio/Shutterstock, 38–39; rybin/Shutterstock, 3; Toloubaev Stanislav/Shutterstock, 19; tony4urban/Shutterstock, 22; trenaren/Flickr, 44, 47, 92; Cameron Watson/Shutterstock, 14; West Midlands Police/Flickr, 113; Wollertz/Shutterstock, 55; Roman Zhuraviev/Shutterstock, 50–51, 65; Vera Zinkova/Shutterstock, 94; Zuzule/Shutterstock, 24, 42, 49.

Library of Congress Cataloging-in-Publication Data
The American Kennel Club's meet the Rottweiler : the responsible dog owner's handbook.
     pages cm. -- (AKC's meet the breeds series)
 Includes index.
 ISBN 978-1-62008-097-9 (alk. paper)
 1. Rottweiler dog. I. American Kennel Club. II. Title: Meet the Rottweiler.
 SF429.R7A44 2014
 636.73--dc23

                 2013043615

This book has been published with the intent to provide accurate and authoritative information in regard to the subject matter within. While every precaution has been taken in the preparation of this book, the author and publisher expressly disclaim any responsibility for any errors, omissions, or adverse effects arising from the use or application of the information contained herein. The techniques and suggestions are used at the reader's discretion and are not to be considered a substitute for veterinary care or professional advice from a dog trainer. If you suspect a medical or behavior problem, consult a professional.

i-5 Publishing, LLC™
3 Burroughs, Irvine, CA 92618
www.facebook.com/i5press
www.i5publishing.com

Printed and bound in the United States
14 15 16 17   1 3 5 7 9 8 6 4 2

Meet Your New Dog

Welcome to *Meet the Rottweiler*. Whether you're a long-time Rottweiler owner or you've just gotten your first puppy, we wish you a lifetime of happiness and enjoyment with your new pet.

In this book, you'll learn about the history of the breed, receive tips on feeding, grooming, and training, and learn about all the fun you can have with your dog. The American Kennel Club and i5 Press hope that this book serves as a useful guide on the lifelong journey you'll take with your canine companion.

Owned and cherished by hundreds of thousands across America, Rottweilers make wonderful companions and also enjoy taking part in a variety of dog sports, including conformation (dog shows), obedience, agility, tracking, and carting.

Thousands of Rottweilers have also earned the AKC Canine Good Citizen® certification by demonstrating their good manners at home and in the community. We hope that you and your Rottweiler will become involved in AKC events, too! Learn how to get involved at www.akc.org/events or find a training club in your area at www.akc.org/events/trainingclubs.cfm.

We encourage you to connect with other Rottweiler owners on the AKC website (www.akc.org), Facebook (www.facebook.com/ americankennelclub), and Twitter (@akcdoglovers). Also visit the website of the American Rottweiler Club (www.amrottclub.org), the national parent club for the Rottweiler, to learn about the breed from reputable exhibitors and breeders.

Enjoy *Meet the Rottweiler!*
Sincerely,

Dennis B. Sprung
AKC President and CEO

Contents

CHAPTER ONE

The Rottweiler
Commitment

Robust, powerful, and loyal, the Rottweiler has strong protective instincts that have been used in modern times to serve humankind in various capacities. Due to the breed's size, strength, and instincts, owning a Rottweiler is a tremendous responsibility that must be assumed with seriousness. The national parent club, the American Rottweiler Club, warns new owners, "For us, it is the best breed in the world, but it is not a dog for everyone." A Rottweiler who has been properly bred, trained, and socialized can become a beloved, trusted companion.

Established in 1971, the American Rottweiler Club is the national breed club of the Rottweiler, a Member Club of the American Kennel Club. Its purpose is "to encourage and promote the quality breeding of purebred Rottweilers and to protect and advance the interests of the breed." While the members of the ARC engage in various pursuits with their dogs, from showing and therapy to Schutzhund and carting, they are all united in their love and respect of the breed. For more information about the ARC, visit www.amrottclub.org or the club's Facebook page.

Without socialization and physical and mental activity, however, the bored Rottweiler can be a real challenge.

NOT FOR EVERYONE

During the 1990s, the Rottweiler breed soared to the number-two position in American Kennel Club registrations, an alarming statistic when one considers that the Rottweiler is not the kind of dog most dog owners can handle, train, and accommodate. The Rottweiler quite simply is not the breed for everyone. Rottweilers require an experienced dog owner to handle, train, and accommodate the breed's size, strength, and intelligence.

No one will deny that a well-bred Rottweiler is a loyal and loving companion, but he is also a large, powerful dog, whose natural instincts are to protect his home and family. Although the Rottweiler isn't one of the largest guard dogs—the Mastiff, Neapolitan Mastiff, and Great Dane are giants in comparison—he is solid muscle and determination. With little effort, a Rottweiler can knock over a full-grown adult; with no effort, a child or senior.

Given the breed's impressive physical stature and its intense focus, the question arises, "Are Rottweilers aggressive?" The answer is, they certainly can be, and their strong territorial instincts can lead them to defend their properties and owners. A Rottweiler will not hesitate to stand up to an intruder when the need arises. Owners must commit to properly socializing the young puppy in order to be in control of their dog. Bursting with confidence and bravura, a Rottweiler can bully his owner, so early training must instill in the puppy what the pecking order of the house will be. Rottweiler ownership is not for those inexperienced with guardian breeds. This is a serious and powerful dog who demands an owner who is committed to caring for, training, and controlling his or her dog for life. Serious training and socialization are necessary components of Rottweiler ownership.

According to the breed standard, "The Rottweiler is basically a calm, confident, and courageous dog with a self-assured aloofness that does not lend itself to immediate and indiscriminate friendships." Those qualities well describe a reliable sentry, someone you'd like to hire to protect you day and night. Rottweilers don't make friends quickly, so strangers should not enter the Rottweiler's house unannounced. An unknown person, even one familiar with the breed or other guardian breeds, should be told that a Rottweiler in his home environment is on duty 24 hours a day. Once a Rottweiler accepts you as a friend, you are assured a friend for life. Rottweilers have long memories and don't forget friends, even if they're infrequent visitors.

Rottweilers live for fun, and this athletic dog enjoys active sports with his favorite humans. Introduce the puppy to low-contact games that do not involve jumping or galloping. Owners must also resist the urge to play rough with their Rottweilers, as such roughhousing can encourage aggression in any breed. It is not advisable to let a Rottweiler overcome his owner even in play.

ROTTWEILERS AND LITTLE PEOPLE

Toddlers and small children are not a good match for the exuberant Rottweiler. Even a Rottweiler puppy can be too much dog, and the puppy's bursts of energy can easily

topple a small child. Young children tend to be more erratic in their movement and frequently screech and squeal in play and distress. Such behavior and noise-making can stimulate the puppy's bite instinct, which can be upsetting to the child or even painful. School-age children, no younger than eight or nine years old, however, are more dependable with the Rottweiler. The American Rottweiler Club believes that the Rottweiler is an outstanding family dog who is good with children, "a combination protector and playmate." No dog as large as the Rottweiler can be left unsupervised with children. The dog is meant to be a protector and companion, but not a nanny. Supervision by a responsible adult is a must.

Remember that in addition to being a protector the Rottweiler is also a herding dog, and it's not uncommon for Rottweilers to regard children as their charges (aka stock!). When working on a farm or ranch, Rottweilers nip at the heels of recalcitrant sheep and cattle in order to move them; once the stock is moving along, the dog stays close and does not continue to nip. A Rottweiler in herding mode—attempting to block, bump, and circle—can be dangerous for children who think the dog is playing games. Early training will discourage the Rottweiler from treating your kids as goats (or ducks or sheep).

Again, adult supervision and common sense rule the day. Be an alert parent for your kids and your dog. Children must never be allowed to harass the Rottie, even though the breed is more durable than most breeds. Too often dog owners forget that their dogs are dogs, and a dog that is hurt will feel that he has to protect himself. As tough as Rotties are, they are not built for teasing and tugging (no animal is). It's just instinct.

Did You Know ?

The Rottweiler in the United States enjoyed moderate popularity in the 1970s but began the rise in the 1980s. By the 1990s, the breed reached the apex of its popularity, number two in the country, according to AKC statistics.

A well-bred, well-socialized Rottweiler can be a loving and protective companion for a family with school-age children.

Likewise, Rottweilers should not be permitted to jump on or knock over children. Rotties love to play and their exuberance is too much for small children to handle. Keep in mind, too, that dogs and kids play with very similar toys, and stuffed animals and balls can lead to avoidable exchanges.

The truth of the matter is that all Rottweilers are unique, and some dogs adapt better to children than others. Early socialization with children helps the Rottweiler to accept and respect little people, and most dogs learn to endure rough play; some dogs, however, have no patience with children's grabbing and pulling. Always carefully monitor any interactions between kids and your Rottweiler.

DISCIPLINE AND TRAINING

Training a dog as large and powerful animal as the Rottweiler is not optional: it is mandatory. If you are seeking out an easycare pet that doesn't demand training, then you are better off getting a couple of cats: the Rottweiler is not for you. If, however, you admire the strength and nobility of this breed, then you must commit to training your puppy, beginning the day he comes to your home.

Not every dog owner has the inclination to train a dog. Oftentimes owners of smaller breeds opt not to obedience train their dogs, which can lead to spoiled dogs who yip and nip with no regard to the humans around them. While any dog bite can do damage—even that of a Pomeranian or Chihuahua—a larger dog can do more harm, thereby making the training and control of such a dog mandatory.

We cannot overemphasize how serious is the owner's obligation for training the Rottweiler. Here's a wake-up call for most of us: in all likelihood, your Rottweiler will grow up to be stronger than you are. Making a strong impression on your puppy (before he weighs 100 pounds) that you are the one in charge is the best idea you're going to take away from this book.

Words like "discipline" and "reprimand" may be frowned upon in certain training-school circles, but the American Rottweiler Club doesn't shy away from saying that "it is very important to establish control over your dog." The club believes that any large, protective dog requires some form of structured training on a day-to-day basis. By no means does that advocate rough handling of the dog, and most Rottweilers can be controlled through verbal cues only. The dog must understand that there are limits on his behavior, and that you (the one in charge) is to be respected and heeded. Positive training, using lots of praise and rewards, is the key to bonding with and training your dog. While physical corrections are occasionally warranted for some strong-willed dogs, physical control does not require overly tough methods. Harsh training methods can impair a dog's trust in his owner, and that trust is crucial to training the Rottweiler. It is best to work with an experienced trainer to learn effective training methods and appropriate techniques for discipline if necessary.

Fortunately, the Rottweiler has a strong desire to please his owner, and once he understands the meaning of a command, he will obey it without hesitation. According to the ARC, discipline, which may be required on very stubborn dog, must always be "consistent, fair, and firm, without being rough." Rottweilers are very sensitive and perceptive, and they require confident and kind owners who have the time to train them properly.

CAVE CANEM

Perhaps the Rottweiler's far-off ancestors in Rome once slept under a sign that said "*Cave canem*" (the Latin phrase for "Beware the dog"). The Rottweiler is a formidable guard dog, and it is the breed's muscle and heart that continually attract newcomers

Obedience should be a lifetime commitment for responsbile Rottweiler owners. Consider joining an obedience club in your area to brush up your dog's command repertory.

to the breed. When a Rottweiler voices a warning ("property guarded by a Rottweiler who means business"), smart intruders retreat. A full-throated, resonant Rottweiler bark is spine-chilling and all the "guard work" most Rotties will ever have to do. The Rottweiler has the "metal" needed to back up his bark, and he will defend his property and family with determination if necessary. The stronger you bond with your Rottweiler, the more ardently he will protect you. Experienced trainers will agree that owners should become trusted masters and earn their Rottweiler's love; trainers who use harsh methods to make their dogs fear them are only destroying their relationship with their dogs. No lasting relationship can be based on fear.

Meet the Rottweiler

AKC Meet the Breeds®, hosted by the American Kennel Club, is a great place to see Rottweilers, as well as more than one hundred and fifty other dog breeds. Not only can you see dogs and puppies of all sizes, you can also talk to experts in each of the breeds. Meet the Breeds features demonstration rings to watch events for law-enforcement K9s, grooming, agility, and obedience. You also can browse the more than one hundred vendor booths for every imaginable product for you and your pet.

It's great fun for the whole family. AKC Meet the Breeds takes place in the fall in New York City. For more information, check out www.meetthebreeds.com.

The Rottweiler naturally perceives danger and can often instinctively distinguish between friend and foe. He will remember your friends and greet them with enthusiasm. Strangers are well advised to announce themselves before attempting to enter a home that is inhabited by a Rottweiler. Owners should post signage (in English!) to warn visitors, delivery people, and in-laws that a large dog resides here!

When well socialized and properly introduced, a Rottweiler can share his home with a family cat or an older dog. It is more of a challenge to introduce a Rottweiler who has been an "only dog" to new pets. Generally, male Rotties get along better with females and are less tolerant of other boys. Females can be welcoming of either sex, though some females will not accept other female dogs in their households.

A MEMBER OF THE FAMILY

Adding a dog to your home in essence is expanding your family, and the Rottweiler puppy will want to become an integral part of yours. Rotties love time spent with their humans and crave attention. This breed should be as affectionate and loyal as it is courageous and confident. Every member of your family should be in favor of the choice of a Rottweiler. The puppy will want to count everyone in the household as his own, young and old, male and female.

As seriously as the Rottweiler accepts his duty as a sentinel for his home and family, he cannot be left alone outside for hours on end. Like any companion animal, the Rottweiler becomes lonely and bored and may feel dejected. When allowed into the home to spend time with the family, the Rottweiler blossoms into a fun-loving, entertaining dog who is a joy to have around. A Rottweiler without stimulation and regular attention can become a black and tan nightmare. They must be house dogs.

Rottweilers enjoy spending time outdoors as much as any vigorous working breed, so be sure to provide him with a securely fenced yard. A six-foot fence is necessary to contain this athletic canine. It is highly inadvisable to chain a dog

A True Multi-Purpose Dog

Over the years, the Rottweiler has served humankind in many capacities. The breed has long been prized as a companion and all-around working dog. In Germany the dog was originally used as a cattle drover but also served as a cart puller for farmers and butchers. In modern times, while the Rottweiler works as a military and police dog, he also serves mankind as a search and rescue dog, an arson-detection dog, a therapy dog, a service dog, and, of course, a competition dog for shows and trials.

The "butcher's dog," as the breed was once known, has a natural affinity for making bovine acquaintances.

outdoors, even for short periods. Rottweiler owners should never allow their dogs to run loose. Such a large dog can easily frighten neighbors or do damage to their property. The Rottweiler's lack of fear extends to automobiles, so it's critical to keep an unrestrained dog away from roadways and parking lots.

If you do not have a fenced-in yard, or live in the city, you will have to commit to taking your Rottweiler on daily walks a few times a day. The length of your walks will increase as your puppy grows, but don't overdo it at first. Puppies aren't built for mile-long jogs. Walking is ideal time to reinforce basic training and to bond more closely with your dog.

ROTTWEILERS ON THE FARM

Although the image of the Rottweiler as a police dog is commonplace today, the breed was once admired as a multi-purpose farm dog. Well documented, too, is the Rottweiler's role as a butcher's dog, driving cattle to market. The dog's ability to drive cattle translated easily to herding work on the farm, and the Rottweiler could be used to herd a variety of stock, from cattle to ducks.

Owners today find that Rottweilers adapt easily to a life in the country, and the breed excels at many farm tasks, according to the editors of *Hobby Farms* magazine. The breed is easier to train than many large working dog types and is more family-oriented. In addition to herding livestock, the Rottweiler can also be a terrific flock guardian. It's all in the training.

Rottweiler puppies raised on farms must be acclimated to the livestock daily. It takes time and daily reinforcement to focus the Rottweiler to the desired task at hand. Apparently nothing is more fun for a Rottie pup than chasing chickens, which is entertaining for everyone except the chickens. With persistence and treats (not chicken flavored), this behavior can be discouraged.

INSURANCE

Anti-Rottweiler policies have hurt lovers of this breed for many years now, and owners sometimes have found it difficult to secure insurance on their homes, condos, and apartments. Many insurance companies refuse to offer Rottweiler owners homeowner or rental insurance, which usually includes dog-bite coverage. Some insurance companies require owners of certain breeds to provide documentation from a vet or trainer to vouch for the dog's good behavior.

The Association of Pet Dog Trainers (APDT), comprised entirely of dog professionals, believes that insurance companies' designating "certain breeds as inherently dangerous implies to the public that behavior is not effectively influenced, positively or negatively, by training." Of course, training by responsible owners is the only way to prevent unwanted behavior in dogs.

Like the parent club, the AKC continually fights against breed-specific laws and "believes that insurance companies should determine coverage of a dog-owning household based on a dog's deeds, not a dog's breed." The APDT echoes this sentiment: "Singling out and publicly demonizing certain breeds as dangerous is unfair, discriminatory, and does an immense disservice to those breeds and the people who care about them."

The more responsible every Rottweiler owner is, the less likely further breed-specific legislation will arise. Become the model good dog owner. Be informed of laws in your community, including leash and pooper-scooper, and be sure to keep your dog's license and rabies vaccination up to date. Attend obedience classes with your Rottweiler and earn the AKC Canine Good Citizen award.

"In fact," AKC sums it up, "insurance companies should consider a dog an asset, a natural alarm system whose bark may deter intruders and prevent potential theft." And a well-trained Rottweiler in a home is a major asset!

If you are seriously considering the Rottweiler, a good first step is to join the American Rottweiler Club. The national parent club is for everyone who cares about this breed, and you will learn everything you need to know about the breed, its characteristics, standard, as well as how to find a breeder and select a puppy. The ARC also offers advice on where to obtain insurance.

At a Glance ...

"The best breed in the world" isn't the dog for everyone. Only experienced dog owners who are willing and able to socialize, train, and control their dogs deserve to call themselves Rottweiler owners.

. . . .

An adaptable working dog, the Rottweiler counts fans and friends around the world who prize the breed for its loyalty, protective instincts, and intelligence. He's also a handsome, funny, and affectionate companion.

. . . .

The Rottie is not the ideal dog for a family with young children; though for older children who respect the dog, the breed is a highly valued "protector and playmate."

. . . .

The Rottweiler is a versatile working dog, whose background began as a farm dog, butcher's dog, and cart puller. Today his résumé includes police dog, military dog, home companion and guard, show dog, therapy dog, and competition dog. You name it, the Rottie can do it!

CHAPTER TWO

Making the **Black** and **Tan**

What does the Rottweiler have in common with the Manchester Terrier and the Black and Tan Coonhound? These are the three AKC breeds that may only be shown in the black and tan color pattern. Sure, lots of other breeds can be black and tan, but they all come in other colors too. There are blue and red Doberman Pinschers, ruby and tricolored Cavaliers, and dappled Dachshunds, but the Rottiwiler is

A masterpiece in black and tan, every Rottweiler should have his rich mahogany spots and markings in the exact places, as described in the breed standard.

exhibited only in one color pattern: "always black with rust to mahogany markings."

The breed standard is very specific in its description of the breed's color, noting that the demarcation between the two colors must be clearly defined and indicating exactly where the markings should be, from eyebrows to toes. "The markings should be located as follows: a spot over each eye; on cheeks; as a strip around each side of muzzle, but not on the bridge of the nose; on throat; triangular mark on both sides of prosternum; on forelegs from carpus downward to the toes; on inside of rear legs showing down the front of the stifle and broadening out to front of rear legs from hock to toes, but not completely eliminating black from rear of pasterns; under tail; black penciling on toes." As detailed as that list of markings may seem, the laws of genetics govern where these markings occur, and the only real variation that breeders see is how large the markings are in each location. The standard says that no more than 10 percent of the Rottweiler's body color can be tan, though this is only a guideline and no judge has ever tried to do the math!

While the AKC standard states that white markings anywhere on the dog are not allowed (not counting a few stray hairs), it is not uncommon for young puppies to have small white markings on their chest. In time, the white usually turns to tan. White markings on a puppy's feet, however, likely will not darken with age.

As far-fetched as it seems, some disreputable breeders have tried to promote Rottweilers of a different color. The breed standard states that any base color other than black is a show disqualification and lists "straw colored" as a serious fault. If you search hard enough on the Internet, you can find red, white, and blue Rotties as well as brindle, gold, and liver ones. None of these colors is desirable or acceptable for show, though various colors do exist in purebred Rotties.

BEWARE OF GIANTS

In strength, courage, and character, the Rottweiler is a giant among dogs—in pounds and inches, he is only "medium large," as the breed standard describes him. The dog world has its share of giants—think Great Dane and Irish Wolfhound—but the Rottweiler is not intended to be one of those handsome cloud huggers. The male Rottweiler stands 24 to 27 inches at the withers; females, 22 to 25 inches. The standard indicates that mid-range between these sizes is preferred. While the standard doesn't indicate weight, proportionally males are more massive throughout with larger frames and heavier bone than females; the weight range for males is

A PIECE OF HISTORY

The breed's namesake town in Germany was named after the red tile (*rote wil*) from the Roman baths that were discovered there during an excavation in AD 700. A Christian church was being erected on the site, and the town became known as Rottweil. Eventually the town became famous as a trading center, and cattle became an important part of its citizens' livelihoods.

Even young Rottweiler puppies should exhibit the desired compact body, expression, and breed type. A good breeder can predict how his or her puppies will develop to give potential owners an idea of which pups will make the best show candidates.

between 90 to 120 pounds, and for females, 75 to 105 pounds. For comparison sake, judges and breeders in Europe look for a medium-large dog, with the ideal for males being 65 to 66 cm (about 26 inches) and 50 kg (110 pounds).

The standard keeps the Rottweiler's size in perspective by saying, "His compact and substantial build denotes great strength, agility and endurance." A dog who is too large and heavy can neither be compact nor agile. If you encounter a breeder who boasts about his stud dogs tipping the scales at 170 pounds, you're well advised to avoid such a reckless peddler. Such a seller surely is not paying any heed to the breed standard, which lists oversize as a serious fault. At his designated medium-large size, the Rottweiler is already a lot of dog to control—adding another fifty percent to his frame is the recipe for the decimation of this wonderful breed.

WHAT MAKES IT A ROTTWEILER?

We know that the Rottweiler is a medium-large black and tan dog, but what other characteristics define this breed's type. The word *type* refers to the sum of a dog's traits that give the dog a particular look. The AKC defines *type* as "the characteristic qualities distinguishing a breed," and all of these qualities are spelled out in the breed standard. Breeders and judges use the standard as a blueprint for selecting which dogs are closest to the ideal. When a judge selects a Rottweiler as the Best of Breed, he or she is essentially saying, "This Rottweiler is the closest to the written standard of all the Rottweilers in this show today." By following the standard, breeders can lock in the desired genetic traits of the breed and improve on subsequent generations.

Standard Terminology from A to Z

The breed standard for the Rottweiler includes a number of terms that may be unfamiliar to newcomers to the breed. Here's a mini-lexicon of terms to make the reading of the standard easier. You can view the complete standard at www.akc.org.

ANGULATION: The angles formed by the bones at their joints; for the forequarters, the shoulders, upper arm, forearm, wrist, pastern, and toes, and for the hindquarters, hip, pelvis, thigh, second thigh, hock, rear pastern and toes

BACKSKULL: Rear portion of the skull

CARPUS: Wrist

DEWCLAW: An extra claw on the inside of the leg

GAIT: Movement; the pattern of footsteps at various rates of speed, each pattern distinguished by a particular rhythm or footfall

HOCK: Ankle

LOIN: The region from rib cage to hip bones

PASTERNS: The metacarpal bones of the leg between the foot and the carpus (front) or the hock (rear)

PROSTERNUM: Point of the breastbone

SET: The placement of the ears on the head, or the junction of the tail and the rump

STIFLE: Knee

TOPLINE: The dog's outline from just behind the withers to the tail set

TUCK-UP: Characterized by markedly shallower body depth at the loin

UNDERLINE: The combined contours of the brisket and the abdominal floor

WITHERS: The highest point of the shoulders, behind the neck

ZYGOMATIC ARCH: Bony ridge that forms the lower part of the eye socket

The standard describes the general appearance, size, proportion, and substance of the dog, as well as the individual anatomical parts (head, neck, topline, body, fore- and hindquarters) as well as coat and color. The standard also describes the desired movement (gait) and the temperament of the breed.

The Rottweiler's head should be of medium length and broad between the ears. A good strong head gives the breed its noble, self-assured expression. The desired pronounced cheek bones and strong upper and lower jaws are required for the gripping power of the dog. When you visit a dog show or watch one on television, take a careful look at the heads on the Rotties. The eyes should be almond shaped and of medium size. They should always be a uniform dark brown color; yellow eyes (called bird of prey eyes) are very undesirable because they give the dog a harsh expression. The breed standard specifically asks that the Rottweiler's eyes have close-fitting lids. While this may seem like a cosmetic request, in fact, it is not: a dog with close-fitting eyelids is better able to work in the dusty environs of a cattle ranch or farm. Loose eyelids expose a dog's eyes to dust and dirt when working.

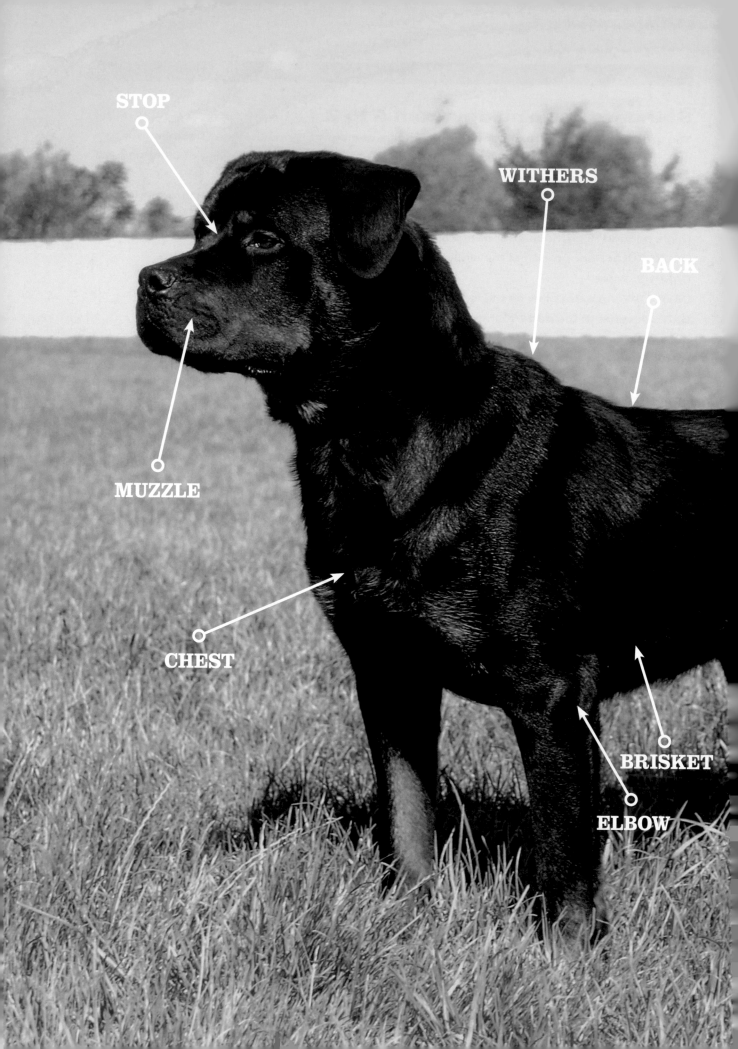

STOP

WITHERS

BACK

MUZZLE

CHEST

BRISKET

ELBOW

CROUP

HIP

LOIN

STIFLE

HOCK

The Rottweiler in Brief

COUNTRY OF ORIGIN:
Germany

ORIGINAL USE:
Butcher's dog; cart puller

GROUP:
Working

AVERAGE LIFE SPAN:
9 to 11 years

COAT:
Straight, coarse, dense, medium length with undercoat

COLOR:
Black with rust to mahogany markings

GROOMING:
Twice-weekly brushing to remove dead coat; daily during twice-annual shedding season

HEIGHT/WEIGHT:
Males—24 to 27 inches; females—22 to 25 inches; 75 to 120 pounds

TRAINABILITY:
Early training critical; positive reinforcement plus firm and fair discipline required to teach the Rottweiler limits and to respect owner's authority

ACTIVITY LEVEL:
High. The Rottweiler thrives on vigorous daily activity and is happiest when doing a job and spending time with his people.

GOOD WITH OTHER PETS:
Early socialization with cats recommended for harmony in the home. Avoid most same-sex pairing of dogs. Small mammals, such as rabbits and guinea pigs, not recommended for Rottweiler homes.

NATIONAL BREED CLUB:
American Rottweiler Club; www. amrottclub.org; Facebook (American Rottweiler Club Information)

RESCUE:
Rottweiler Rescue Network; www.rottnet. net/rottweiler-rescue-foundation

BREED STANDARD FOR THE ROTTWEILER

SIZE, PROPORTION, SUBSTANCE

Dogs—24 inches to 27 inches. Bitches—22 inches to 25 inches, with preferred size being mid-range of each sex. Correct proportion is of primary importance, as long as size is within the standard's range. The length of body, from prosternum to the rearmost projection of the rump, is slightly longer than the height of the dog at the withers, the most desirable proportion of the height to length being 9 to 10. The Rottweiler is neither coarse nor shelly. Depth of chest is approximately fifty percent (50%) of the height of the dog. His bone and muscle mass must be sufficient to balance his frame, giving a compact and very powerful appearance.

HEAD

Of medium length, broad between the ears; forehead line seen in profile is moderately arched; zygomatic arch and stop well developed with strong broad upper and lower jaws. *Eyes* of medium size, almond shaped with well fitting lids, moderately deep-set, neither protruding nor receding. The desired color is a uniform dark brown. *Ears* of medium size, pendant, triangular in shape. Ears are to be set well apart, hanging forward with the inner edge lying tightly against the head and terminating at approximately mid-cheek. *Muzzle*— Bridge is straight, broad at base with slight tapering towards tip. The end of the muzzle is broad with well developed chin. *Nose* is broad rather than round and always black. *Lips*—Always black; corners closed; inner mouth pigment is preferred dark.

NECK

Powerful, well muscled, moderately long, slightly arched and without loose skin.

BODY

The chest is roomy, broad and deep, reaching to elbow, with well pronounced forechest and well sprung, oval ribs. Back is straight and strong. Loin is short, deep and well muscled. Croup is broad, of medium length and only slightly sloping. Underline of a mature Rottweiler has a slight tuck-up. *Tail*—Tail docked short, close to body, leaving one or two tail vertebrae. The set of the tail is more important than length. Properly set, it gives an impression of elongation of topline; carried slightly above horizontal when the dog is excited or moving.

FOREQUARTERS

Shoulder blade is long and well laid back. Upper arm equal in length to shoulder blade, set so elbows are well under body. Legs are strongly developed with straight, heavy bone, not set close together. Feet are round, compact with well arched toes, turning neither in nor out. Nails short, strong and black. Dewclaws may be removed.

HINDQUARTERS

Upper thigh is fairly long, very broad and well muscled. Stifle joint is well turned. Lower thigh is long, broad and powerful, with extensive muscling leading into a strong hock joint. Rear pasterns are nearly perpendicular to the ground. Feet are somewhat longer than the front feet, turning neither in nor out, equally compact with well arched toes. Dewclaws must be removed.

COAT

Outer coat is straight, coarse, dense, of medium length and lying flat. Undercoat should be present on neck and thighs, but the amount is influenced by climatic conditions. Undercoat should not show through outer coat. The coat is shortest on head, ears and legs, longest on breeching. The Rottweiler is to be exhibited in the natural condition with no trimming.

--excerpted from the American Rottweiler Club breed standard--

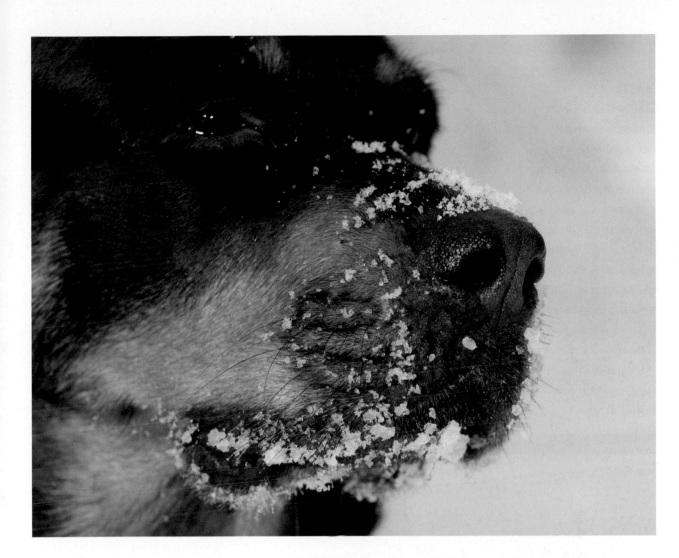

The dog's triangular ears are medium sized and carried at the level of the top of the skull, appearing to make the skull look broader. You may also see a head with too much excess skin, but the standard asks for a dry forehead, meaning no wrinkles except when the dog is alert. There should also be a well-defined stop (the indentation between the eyes right above the nose). A dog who lacks the desired stop may appear "houndy" or coarse and resemble a Bullmastiff. The Rottweiler's muzzle is straight and broad at the base, slightly tapering to the tip. The muzzle should be one-third the overall length of the head. A dog with an overly long muzzle and a narrow head might resemble a snipy Labrador Retriever.

The Rottweiler's head sits on a powerful, well-muscled neck that is moderately long. When you view the Rottweiler standing still, its back should be firm and level, with a straight topline from withers to croup. When the dog starts to move, the back should remain level and practically motionless. The dog's tail, which is traditionally docked, must be set to give the impression of continuing the topline.

A Rottweiler's body length to height ratio should be 9:10, though females are sometimes a bit longer. The dog's chest should be deep and broad, and its proportions play an important role in the correct appearance of the breed. The standard says, "Depth of chest is approximately 50 percent of the height of the dog," which means that a dog who stands 26 inches at the withers should have a depth of brisket of 13 inches.

"Broad" well describes the Rottweiler's head, muzzle, and nose, as well as his appeal around the world.

The Dominator

Confident and courageous, Rottweilers can be dominant dogs but they are not overly aggressive toward other dogs, especially when they meet them on neutral ground. The breed's territorial instincts may result in a Rottweiler's being intolerant of another dog, particularly of the same sex.

So as not to hinder the dog's agile movement, the shoulders should be well laid back without being overly muscled. The front legs should be straight and heavily boned and not too close together. The angulation of the hindquarters balances that of the forequarters and should not be exaggerated. The dog's pasterns are nearly perpendicular to the ground, which means that the wrists should be straight and not bent. The upper thighs of the rear legs are broad and should be visibly well muscled.

The Rottweiler's front feet are described as round and compact with well-arched toes, which is to say catlike, and the hind feet are somewhat longer than the front, but also tightly knuckled.

The standard describes the Rottweiler's movement as "trotting," indicating that the gait should be balanced, harmonious, and powerful. When trotting, the front and rear feet should be coordinated, with the legs converging under the body toward a center line as the speed increases.

The Rottweiler should have a straight, dense and coarse outer coat and is shown in a natural state with no trimming.

WORKING DOGS

In 1931, the Rottweiler was accepted into the AKC Working Group, a most fitting categorization for this versatile dog who has performed various tasks, such as cart pulling, cattle droving, and guarding. Even though the Rottweiler is an able herding dog, moving livestock is not the breed's principal function, so the breed was not moved to the Herding Group upon its formation in 1983. That said, the Rottweiler is not the only breed in the Working Group with herding abilities: the Giant and Standard Schnauzers, Bernese Mountain Dog, and Samoyed have all been utilized for livestock and, like the Rottweiler, are eligible to compete in AKC herding trials.

Many of the world's most highly regarded guardian breeds are members of the Working Group, including the Boxer, Doberman Pinscher, Mastiff, Neapolitan Mastiff, and Bullmastiff. With the group's two Swiss dogs, the Greater Swiss Mountain Dog and Bernese Mountain Dog, the Rottweiler shares a cart-pulling heritage. Other unique breeds in the Working Group have performed tasks as diverse as guarding temples, working for the military, and retrieving fishing nets, namely the Tibetan Mastiff, Black Russian Terrier, and Portuguese Water Dog.

At a Glance ...

As colorful as the Rottie's personality is, his coat is not: this is a black and tan-only breed. The standard indicates exactly where every marking on the Rottweiler's body should occur.

. . . .

A medium-large dog with a compact, substantial build, the Rottweiler is not a giant breed, standing no more than 27 inches at the shoulders and tipping the scales at 120 pounds.

. . . .

Understanding the breed standard is key to being able to recognize a well-bred Rottweiler. Whether you're seeking a companion or show dog (or both), you want a Rottweiler who well represents his breed, in mind, body, and spirit.

. . . .

Having joined the AKC Working Group in 1931, the Rottweiler's quintessential versatility makes him an exemplary member of this diverse group.

CHAPTER THREE

The Search for a Puppy

When selecting a Rottweiler, proceed with caution and patience. This is a very important acquisition, and you will be investing more than the purchase price of the puppy. Your commitment of time and emotion outweighs the financial investment, and you will be entering into a ten-year (or more!) contract with this noble animal. Unlike a new SUV or laptop, you cannot "upgrade" your model in a few years: Rottweilers are for keeps. The loyalty and affection that your Rottweiler shares with you and

What Does It Take to Own a Rottweiler?

- Owner must be physically fit and able to handle a large, powerful dog
- Owner must be willing to train and discipline the dog
- Owner must be willing to invest the time into caring for and training the dog and be prepared for a ten-year commitment
- Owner must have enough space to accommodate the dog and ideally a fenced-in backyard

your whole family are the payback for spending the time to find the right breeder and puppy.

ARE YOU SURE YOU'RE READY FOR A ROTTWEILER?

The American Rottweiler Club emphasizes that this magnificent, noble breed is not for everyone, and many people who are impressed by and enamored of this breed do not make suitable owners for a Rottweiler. Consider your owner qualifications carefully before you reach out to a breeder to purchase a puppy.

1. Do you have the time to give to a dog? A dog is a major imposition on an owner's time, requiring walking, feeding, training, and so forth. Having time for a dog does not mean that you cannot work and own a dog. Your pet will need quality time, just as a child does. He must be fed two times a day and exercised several times a day. You must work with him to have an obedient, mannerly dog.

2. Is your yard securely fenced in? You cannot leave the Rottweiler tied out on the porch or allow him to roam free. He must have a secure area in which to run and exercise. A yard that's big enough for ball playing is ideal. Remember, it is your responsibility to keep the yard clean of feces. When walking your dog, it is essential to carry a plastic bag or two to pick up droppings.

3. Are you strong and smart enough to handle an adult Rottweiler? An adult Rottweiler is a strong, assertive canine with an independent streak. He requires an experienced dog owner who can demonstrate to the dog that he or she is confident enough to be in charge. Rotties are bright and perceptive too, which means they can outwit a dimwit and size up phonies with little effort.

4. Are you certain that your community allows you to own a Rottweiler? Unfortunately, a number of towns and cities have passed breed-specific laws that restrict and/or ban the ownership of certain breeds. Your local council may not allow certain breeds in the area and the Rottweiler just may be one of these breeds. Visit http://rott-n-chatter.webs.com for an update on breed-specific laws in US cities. Speaking of neighborhoods, you may want to let your neighbors know that you are adding a Rottweiler to your household. Speak intelligently about the breed and reassure them that you are purchasing your puppy from a responsible breeder. When the time comes, make sure to introduce the puppy to your neighbors.

5. Do you have sufficient indoor space for a Rottweiler? Unlike some more sedentary large breeds, the Rottweiler will not be content in a studio apartment or small mobile home. Rotties are active dogs and enjoy playing indoors as well as out. On a rainy day, you will need some inside footage for your Rottweiler to stretch

his legs—or you'll have to buy a poncho for you and the dog to rough it in wet weather.

6. Do you have young children? Children under ten years of age are not ideal companions for a breed as heavy and strong as the Rottweiler. We discussed children in detail in the first chapter of this book.

BREEDERS FIRST

An experienced breeder invests a great deal of time and commitment into the planning of a litter and the raising of the puppies. A breeder will ask a fair price for a puppy from the litter, but very often breeding is not a profitable endeavor, even for the breeders who have stellar reputations for producing top-quality puppies. A good breeder will not pressure you to purchase a puppy and does not badmouth other breeders and kennels. Instead, an experienced, confident breeder will encourage you to research the breed, to meet other breeders and owners, and to attend an AKC dog show to see the dogs in action. Any breeder who doesn't welcome questions or who doesn't allow you inside his or her home should be considered.

When selecting a breeder, look for a breeder who:

- is knowledgeable about the breed and has bred more than a couple of generations of his or her line
- can clearly explain why he or she selected the dam and sire and what he or she hoped to achieve with this particular breeding
- registers the litter with the American Kennel Club, participates in AKC shows and/or trials, and is a member of the American Rottweiler Club and possibly a regional Rottweiler club
- is personally involved with the socialization and raising of the puppies
- is eager to assist you with the details of getting started with the puppy, offering you tips on feeding, training, health, and supplies
- sells puppies that are eight weeks of age or older, and doesn't ship pups younger than that

The sound, even temperament of a Rottweiler dam is evident when watching her interact with her litter. This dam has her paws full with a brood of hungry babies.

Find a Breeder Online

An easy way to start your search for a qualified breeder is to visit the AKC website at www.akc.org. Under "Owners," select the tab for "Find a Puppy." This tab will bring you to a page for you to select a breed (Rottweiler!), input your zip code, and select a mileage range (from 50 to 500 miles to "Nationwide"). Select "50" and cross your fingers that there is a breeder close to your home. The breeders on the AKC website are not officially endorsed by the club, but they are categorized by "AKC Breeder of Merit" (a major plus), "Member of AKC-licensed or member club" (always a plus), and "Seller of AKC-registrable puppies" (worth investigating). If no breeder comes up within 100 or even 200 miles of your home, you should visit the American Rottweiler Club's website for breeder referrals. There are also local all-breed dog clubs and rescue groups that may be able to assist you in finding a puppy or older dog.

- is professional and businesslike when discussing the price of the puppy and the conditions of the sale, providing all terms in writing
- has the puppies checked over by a veterinarian and has performed health screenings for hips, elbows, eyes, and heart, as recommended by the American Rottweiler Club

MEETING THE BREEDER

When visiting the breeder, don't be afraid to ask questions. A good breeder expects that you will be brimming with questions and will be pleased that you are being conscientious. Doing your homework about the breed and wanting to find a reputable breeder are good things. Get the breeder's opinion on the breed. Ask him or her about the breed's temperament and what training methods work best in his or her experience. How long does it take to house-train the puppy? How much exercise does the puppy require? Find out when his or her puppies begin to act like adults and how large the males and females become? Ask how often you should groom the puppy and whether or not the dogs bark a lot. Ask about health screening of both parents (and grandparents). The breeder will be glad to see that you're being thorough in your preparation for becoming a Rottweiler owner.

If you have aspirations of showing or competing in trials with the puppy, you should share these with the breeder. If you're looking for a puppy to exhibit in a dog show or to compete in obedience or tracking, the breeder will advise you about which puppies would make the best candidates. If you're hoping to get involved with therapy work or looking for a companion for your (not too young) children, let the breeder know. Since many people seek the Rottweiler as both a companion and working dog, most breeders will advise you about the importance of socialization and early training, recommending training classes as the best first step.

Breeders should be knowledgeable about the genetics of their dogs, and if you ask the breeder about the puppy's pedigree, you're likely to learn more than you bargain for. Breeders love to talk about their dogs, especially the ones that they love enough to breed. The breeder should have very specific reasons for having paired together this particular dam and sire. Be ready to hear buzz words like "soundness," "balance," "structure," "movement," and "temperament." All of these are ideal components of a well-made Rottweiler, whether that puppy is going to grow to become an obedience competitor, a show dog, a family pet, or all three.

Don't be put off by a breeder who uses the terms "pet quality" and "show potential." A pet-quality Rottweiler is not like "seconds" at a factory outlet, instead it is as sound, healthy, and friendly as any puppy in the litter. By comparison, the show-potential puppy exhibits certain stronger characteristics described in the breed standard. Usually these characteristics are of little importance to the pet owner, but if you're interested in showing the puppy, you'll want to purchase the puppy that the breeder believes will develop into a really good representative of the breed. Without a doubt, the "show potential" puppy will cost more than a "pet quality" puppy.

An experienced breeder, someone who has bred his or her line of dogs for a number of years, has seen the puppies grow up and can predict how puppies will develop. Good breeders take advantage of dog shows as the testing ground for their stock, which is still the intended purpose of dog shows. Judges review a breeder's stock to weigh in on which dogs are best for reproducing the next generation of dogs. Many breeders show their own dogs or work with professional handlers who exhibit their dogs regularly.

If you visit a large all-breed dog show, you'll be able to see puppies from various breeders all in the same place. Dog shows offer matches for puppies three months of age and older, and puppy classes for puppies six months of age or older. If you can find a Rottweiler specialty show (a show for Rotties only), you should be able to watch a puppy sweepstakes class and get to meet lots of Rottweiler folk and their dogs. There's no better place than a dog show to begin your puppy search.

Due to the ongoing efforts of the American Kennel Club and the commitment of reputable Rottweiler breeders, potential health concerns of the breed are well documented and being reduced with each generation. Breeders should screen all of

DNA Mapping

Advances in modern science to map the canine genome potentially can lead conscientious breeders toward healthier dogs. Many breed clubs are encouraging breeders to participate in testing, and today with the completion of canine genome mapping, some 500 hereditary disorders, affecting purebred and mixed-breed dogs, have been described, 100 of which have genetic markers. This type of screening allows breeders to identify carriers of particular disorders merely by the presence of only a gene or two. Of course, not every dog carrying a gene will develop the disorder, but these DNA tests provide valuable information to breeders as they choose dogs to breed.

Did You Know?

In addition to nipping at the heels of cattle, Rottweilers had to develop other methods of convincing uncooperative cows to move it along. Staring, or eyeing, the stock is a method used by Collies as well as Rottweilers to intimidate the animals to keep their distance and heed the dog's directions.

their breeding stock for congenital problems that affect all purebred and mixed-breed dogs. Hip and elbow dysplasia, two hereditary diseases that affect the joints of large dogs, are evaluated through X-rays and registered with the Orthopedic Foundation for Animals (OFA). Only dogs who have been certified as free of dysplasia should be bred. A dog must be two years of age in order to be certified.

The Canine Eye Registration Foundation (CERF) and OFA work with members of the American College of Veterinary Ophthalmologists (ACVO) to maintain a registry for purebred dogs who are clear of hereditary eye diseases, including progressive retinal atrophy, entropion, ectropion, and cataracts. Screening for heart conditions is also a must.

Expect that the breeder will have questions for you about your lifestyle, work commitments, children, home and yard, and experience with dogs. Reputable breeders will not place a puppy with a new owner simply because he or she can afford the price of the puppy. Breeders have invested many hours and much effort into planning and producing the litter, and money should not be their

A puppy inherits more than his good looks from his parents. A sweet, friendly temperament and, to some extent, good manners are gifts from mom.

primary concern. They want to place their puppies into good homes with responsible owners who are going to commit to giving their Rotties the best lives possible. Breeders are heartbroken when they find out an owner surrendered one of their pups, though most breeders will accept the puppy (or adolescent or adult) back if the owner decides it's not working out. A good breeder stays in touch with puppy buyers and wants updates on the puppy's growth and development. He or she is also available to answer questions and to offer advice on training, diet, health concerns, and anything else that comes up. The more interested the breeder is in you at the interview, the more committed he or she will be to the puppy and you further down the road.

MEETING THE LITTER AND CHOOSING A PUPPY

Once you've found a breeder whose experience and approach appeal to you, you should be able to visit his or her home or kennel to meet the litter. Many breeders raise puppies in their homes, though some may have an auxiliary building on their property designated as a kennel. How the puppies are kept will tell you a lot about the breeding establishment. Is the puppies' area clean and good-smelling or is it neglected and foul-smelling? Rottweilers typically have large litters, and more puppies means more work for the dam and more mess.

You should be able to meet the dam of the litter, who may not be as perky and carefree as her normal self. Rearing a litter of five to ten bouncy Rottie pups is tough work for a mom. While dams are typically protective of their babies, she should still be approachable and warm up to visitors after a short while. Remember that Rottweilers aren't as eager to make friends as Goldens or Beagles—there's a natural aloofness about them upon first meeting. If the dam of the litter is not present, that is a cause for concern, especially if you're purchasing a puppy who is seven or eight weeks of age or younger.

Be sure also to ask the breeder about the sire of the litter. It is not at all uncommon for the sire to not be on the premises. Ask to see photos of him and inquire about his temperament, background. and health clearances. Most breeders will not breed their bitches to a dog who has not proven his merit in the show ring or at trials. Hopefully, the sire has a title or two added to his name.

The puppies should be clean and smell like puppies (there's no way to describe it: you just know it when you smell it). The breeder should have trimmed the puppies' toenails and cleaned their faces to greet visitors. You should see that the puppies' noses are moist, their coats glistening, and their little square bodies covered in flesh over their ribs. The breeder may show you only two or three puppies, as he or she may not wish to show you puppies that are already spoken for.

TEMPERAMENT TESTING

Many breeders participate in formal temperament tests with their Rottweilers. While this isn't mandatory, it shows that the breeders are serious about producing dogs with sound, reliable temperaments. Formal temperament tests are offered by the American Temperament Test Society (ATTS), whose motto is "A sound mind in a sound body." If the breeder has participated in these tests on the dam and/or sire, he or she should be able to show you the score sheet for you to determine whether the parents are temperamentally sound.

The ATTS tests dogs who are at least eighteen months of age, so puppies are not tested. As of February 2013, the ATTS had tested 5,652 Rottweilers, of which 4,751 passed, giving an 84.1% passing rate. The test is a simulated walk through a park or a neighborhood where everyday situations are encountered. Neutral, friendly, and threatening situations are simulated to gauge the dog's reactions to various stimuli. The evaluators are looking for undesirable responses, such as unprovoked aggression, panic without recovery, and strong avoidance. The dog is on a loose lead for the test, which takes about ten minutes to complete.

Some breeders will have the temperaments of their puppies evaluated by a qualified professional, such as a trainer, veterinarian, or another dog breeder. Naturally the breeder will have his or her own observations about the puppies in the litter, and if the breeder has a number of years' experience in breeding dogs, he or she will have a good idea about how the puppies will grow up. It's easy to recognize the outgoing, rowdy puppies from the more serious, introverted puppies. Once the breeder learns about your family, home, and lifestyle, he or she should be able to recommend which pup might be best for you.

When you meet the litter, you can do a few simple tests to discover the puppy personalities on your own. Begin by patting your thigh or snapping your fingers to see which pup comes up to you first. Clap your hands and see whether any puppy shies away from you. Observe how the pups play with one another. Maybe one puppy has a personality that particularly appeals to you. Look for the "middle of the road" puppy, the one who is not bouncing off the walls, climbing over his littermates, or shying away in the corner. Look for the puppy who is content and friendly not wild and dominant. Trust the breeder's instincts and recommendations about the puppies, and together you should be able to narrow down your choice to a puppy who will bring you much joy for years to come.

Hip Dysplasia

A hereditary disease that affects Rottweilers and other large breeds of dog, hip dysplasia (HD) can be very painful for a dog to live with, increasingly so as the dog ages. Only purchase a puppy from a breeder who screens his or her dogs for this disease, thereby increasing your puppy's chance of not developing the disease. Normal (free of HD) adults can produce puppies that will develop dysplasia later in life, so breeders recognize that the disease has other factors beyond genetics. Keeping a dog trim with a proper diet and exercise regimen is recommended, as is avoiding strenuous exercise that can stress a young dog's joints and ligaments.

KÖNIG OR KÖNIGIN?

King or queen...male or female? Some owners know immediately which sex puppy they prefer. Have you thought about whether you want a male or a female? Depending on your situation, one sex may be a better choice for you. Males and females are equally loving and loyal, though each dog is different, and the individual personality of the dog matters more than the sex. Generally speaking, a female Rottie is a sweet companion who is often quite easy to live with, though she can be a bit moody, depending on her whims and hormonal peaks. The male is more even-tempered and bonds closely to his master and family. He is a significantly larger animal, often 2 inches or more taller than the female, and during adolescence can be more physical and exuberant. Both males and females are fairly large and powerful, though it does take more strength and confidence to control a male dog.

A solid foundation in obedience is necessary if you want the dog to respect you as his (or her) leader. An untrained male also can become dominant with people and other dogs. Unneutered males tend to be more territorial, especially with other male dogs, though both male and female Rottweilers can be protective of home and family.

Since many breeders require neutering or spaying of pet Rottweilers, most of the sex-related problems that "whole" dogs encounter will not be factors. If you are considering a Rottweiler for showing, then you will have to contend with the bitch's twice-annual estruses (heat cycles) and the male's year-round search for a willing female in heat. Male Rottweilers, like males of other species, are more interested in reproduction than are females. Males will mark their territory with small amounts of urine (although no amount of urine is that small inside your home), and will wander off in search of a partner (what the Germans call *wanderlust*). *A secure yard is a requirement for all Rottie owners.*

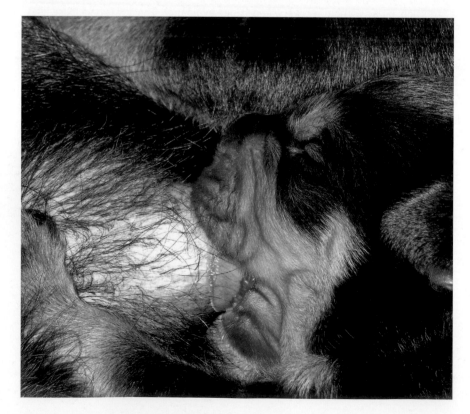

Baby puppies rely on their dams for nourishment, education, and protection—all responsibilities the new owner must assume when taking a puppy home.

Aside from the potential behavioral benefits of neutering and spaying, sexually altered dogs of both sexes may enjoy less risk of some health problems, including reproductive cancers, assuming the procedures are not performed too early in life.

Once you have decided on the most suitable puppy from the litter, an outgoing, happy boy or girl who shows all indications of good health, confidence, and charm, you are on your way to bringing your new acquisition into your household. The excitement is just about to start, but first we have to make sure you, your family, and your home are ready. Read on!

Puppies in the same litter grow at different rates, with male puppies often outgrowing their female siblings.

At a Glance ...

Before beginning your puppy search, ascertain whether you are truly ready to become a Rottweiler owner. Do you have what it takes to train, control, and properly care for this very special dog?

. . . .

A reputable breeder is your best choice for a Rottweiler puppy, but make sure you find the one whose experience and credentials meet your expectations. Contact the American Rottweiler Club for assistance.

. . . .

You will know that you're working with a qualified breeder if he or she has performed the necessary health clearances on the sire and the dam of the litter. Temperament tests are a good plus, too.

. . . .

Once you decide on the preferred sex of your puppy, the breeder should be able to assist you in selecting the best puppy for you, your family, and lifestyle.

CHAPTER FOUR

Puppy Comes Home

There's plenty of homework to do before those tiny mahogany paws hit your kitchen floor running! As fun and exciting as a new puppy can be, it is also a major disruption of your daily routine. Puppies require nearly constant supervision to keep them safe and to safeguard your home and possessions. Before puppy day ("P" day, aptly named) arrives, you need to make sure that you have all of the supplies you're going to need and that your home and yard are puppy-safe. Let's begin with your basic puppy purchases.

Making your new puppy feel at home is one of the joys of being a new owner. Make sensible choices and only purchase safe, well-constructed supplies for your new family member.

SHOPPING FOR PUPPY SUPPLIES

In 2012, Americans spent $12.5 billion dollars on pet supplies and another $20 billion on pet food, according to the American Pet Products Association. Thanks to pet-supply super stores and well-stocked pet shops, box stores, and grocery stores, we are spoiled for choice as we now can find pet supplies everywhere. There is so much good stuff to buy for dogs, and pet owners don't ever seem to skimp on their best friends, even during a recession.

You will soon be contributing to the American pet economy—a total of $52 billion in 2012, which hasn't dipped a single year since the data began being collected in 1994—but proceed wisely and you won't be purchasing the same items over and over. A good buyer's rule for dog supplies is this: purchase the best quality that you can afford the first time so that you don't have to replace it a few years or months down the road.

Bowls

Purchase three large stainless steel feeding bowls. You can keep the third bowl outside for water and use the other two inside for food and water. There are many other options available in the stores, but Rotties don't need fancy plastic bowls, and no rough-and-tumble puppy should be trusted with a ceramic bowl.

Food

You have to have something to put in the bowls, so be sure food is on your list. In Chapter Eight, we will discuss the selection of the best food in detail. Pet stores sell food in various forms: dry (kibble), wet (canned), semi-moist (packages), as well as natural foods (rolls, packages, etc.) and even raw diets. The selection of brands, flavors, and types is overwhelming, but with some guidance from your vet and/or breeder, along with some good information, you'll be sure to make an excellent choice.

Brushes

Do you know which brush to purchase for the Rottweiler puppy? You hear dog people talk about many different coat tools, such as a soft bristle brush, a pin brush, a slicker brush, a rubber grooming mitt, a flea comb, and an undercoat rake. For the puppy, you're best with a combination pin and bristle brush (one side has soft bristles and the other side has pins). For the adult Rottweiler's coat, the undercoat rake will remove the dead hair without disturbing the outer coat. A lot of people like to use the grooming mitt to give the dog a daily onceover, and a flea comb (very thin teeth set close together) is handy for checking for fleas in the coat. A slicker brush (slanted steel pins in a rubber base) is preferred by some owners instead of the undercoat rake, but it's a matter of preference.

Leashes and Collars

An adjustable buckle or clamp collar is the best choice for a fast-growing Rottweiler puppy. As he grows into his paws and gains inches and pounds, his neck expands in circumference. You should be able to comfortably fit two fingers sideways between your dog's neck and his collar. Check it every day to make sure that it's not too tight for him. Collars come in many different materials, but a lightweight nylon web collar is a good starter collar. Look for a 16- to 18-inch collar. As the dog matures, you can invest in a handsome leather collar or a fashionable rhinestone-studded collar. Always be sure the collar is sturdy enough and that the stainless steel rings are securely fastened.

In this day of microchips and GPS collars, here's some good old-fashioned advice: attach an ID tag to your puppy's collar. Your neighbor three blocks away doesn't

Naming Your Rottweiler Puppy

Choosing the right name for your Rottweiler can be challenging, as you want the perfect name to reflect not only the breed's positive characteristics but also the individual puppy's personality. Select a name that suggests the breed's fine character and confidence, and a touch of German pride doesn't hurt either. Here are some popular names for Rotties:

FEMALES: Berta, Betty, Brigitta, Brunnhilde, Dixie, Elizabeth, Elsa, Fricka, Frieda, Gerda, Greta, Gretl, Heidi, Keira, Liesl, Lydia, Maggie, Maxi, Mercedes, Ogla, Reba, Sasha, Sierra, Sieglinde, Sophie, Zelda, Zoe

MALES: Boris, Duke, Erich, Fasolt, Georg, Gunther, Gruber, Harley, Jett, Karl, Leo, Ludwig, Luther, Mac, Magnum, Max, Otto, Parsifal, Rocky, Rogue, Rolf, Rudolf, Samson, Saturn, Siegfried, Tank, Tannhauser, Titan, Trojan, Walter, Woton, Ziff

EITHER: Angel, Blitz, Diesel, Gizmo, Hooch, Kodiak, Midnight, Sasha, Vegas

Once you have selected a name for your puppy, you have to use it when you speak to him, always in a happy, upbeat tone. Never use the pup's name when you are correcting him, as he will associate his name with negative experiences. Say things like "Good, Eva, good" or "That's a handsome boy, Heinrich!" and "Good Knabe, Ludwig." Once you have achieved name recognition, you can begin teaching basic commands.

have a microchip scanner! You can get a tag made online or at a pet shop, and be sure to include your name, cell phone number, and address. The ID tag is your first line of defense to recover a lost dog; the microchip is your safety net.

Accidents can happen, and anything can happen when you're on vacation, at a dog show, or just out and about town.

For training purposes, a choke collar made of nylon or cotton rope is recommended A prong collar (with stainless steel prongs surrounding the collar) is designed to pinch the skin around the dog's neck when the dog pulls. While some trainers use these collars on difficult dogs, they are not recommended for training any dog, especially one as sensitive as the Rottie. Never leave a training collar on an unattended dog.

The leash you purchase should be 6 feet in length (and three-quarter inch in width) and made of cotton or nylon. Most manufacturers make coordinating colors for collars and leashes; there's usually a half dozen colors to choose from as well as patterns.

Provided with guidance and lots of love, your Rottweiler puppy will develop into a smart, obedient companion.

Crate

Owners of large dogs often ignore the standard recommendation to purchase a dog crate. Their resistance is understandable: a dog in a crate can't protect his home and property. Consider that a crate is a training tool for the Rottweiler puppy, and puppies don't protect anything other than their fuzzy toys anyway (an issue we will deal with later). For house-training and travel, a dog crate is indispensable. The crate is the fastest and most effective way to house-train a dog, and it is the safest way to travel with a dog.

An adult Rottweiler will require a crate that is 48 x 36 inches, and most breeders recommend that you purchase an adult-size crate for the puppy. It's a costly investment, but your Rottweiler will use his crate throughout his life as a place

A PIECE OF HISTORY

The first Rottweiler was admitted to the AKC stud book in 1931. The standard was accepted by the American Kennel Club in 1935, and the first American Rottweiler gained his show championship in 1948. However, one of the breed earned his obedience championship in 1939. The American Rottweiler Club was first formed in 1971 and the first national specialty show for the breed was held in 1981.

to sleep in and as a traveling compartment in your (large) car, SUV, or van. The standard wire crate is the best choice, though for airline travel you will need to purchase (or borrow) a fiberglass one.

Gates & Pens

When the puppy first comes home, you will have to restrict him to certain areas of your house. Depending on the floor plan of your house, you may be able to use baby gates (or puppy gates) to limit which rooms the puppy will have access to. If your home doesn't have doorways that can be gated, you can purchase an exercise pen (or ex pen) to be placed in the middle of a room to contain your puppy when you can't keep an eye on him.

Bed

Even though puppies love to sleep in their crates, they also welcome a soft, cushioned bed for naps. Think simple and machine-washable! A bed with a removable cover is a real plus, and usually the polyester-filled cushions can also be thrown in the washing machine. A fleece dog bed is another good option that can be easily laundered. There are literally thousands of dog beds on the market, in all shapes (rectangle, oval, bone, bagel) and sizes, as well as fancy upholstered designs and those designed for practical purposes (heating, cooling, orthopedic for senior dogs, and so forth).

Toys

Play is a serious business when it comes to puppies, so keep your house well stocked with toys! To begin, you can purchase three or four different toys. A retrievable toy, such as a ball or a Frisbee, a plush toy (many of these are shaped like friendly animals), and a rubber or nylon toy for teething (essentially variations on ye old dog bone). If you're looking to add a fourth toy to the cart, then look for a treat-dispensing toy that is a great boredom buster for young dogs.

For your Rottweiler's safety, look for toys that are as indestructible as possible. Avoid toys that are made of latex, can be destroyed easily, or include pieces that can be pulled off.

Treats

Your puppy thinks they're candy, but you know they're training devices. Don't skimp on the treats. Purchase a few different small bags of treats to test out on your puppy. Keep track of which treats he loves, and which ones he just eats. Reserve the favorite treats for the important lessons, such as come, down, and heel.

PUPPY-PROOFING THE HOME AND YARD

Once the puppy comes through the front door, he will want to explore every crevice and corner of your home. Rottweilers can be extremely nosy, and they like to know what's going on. Before the puppy starts sweeping for crumbs, beetles, and dust bunnies, get a head start. Get down on your fours and crawl through the rooms of your house from his vantage point. The house tour begins with the kitchen.

Puppy Kindergarten

Don't hesitate to enroll your Rottweiler puppy into a local puppy class, sometimes called puppy kindergarten. New owners love to show off their new "kids," and your Rottie needs the experience of meeting other pups in a controlled setting like a puppy class. Puppies as young as ten to twelve weeks of age can start in puppy classes to learn some basic household manners, like sitting when greeting a person, walking politely on a leash, and basic behaviors like sit and stay. Choose a class that limits enrollment to eight to ten puppies.

Puppies are curious 24/7, indoors and out. Be aware of what your puppy is investigating and know what things can possibly cause him harm. Certain types of mulch and all fertilizers are harmful to canines.

ROOM-BY-ROOM SAFETY CHECKLIST

Kitchen

☐ Garbage and recyclable container are secure inside a cabinet or their lids are tight fitting.

☐ Cabinets have childproof locks.

☐ Place detergents, polishes, bleach, and all other chemicals in cabinets that can't be reached from the floor.

☐ No electrical cords are dangling from coffee pots, blenders, or other appliances.

☐ There are no gaps between the refrigerator and cabinets or anywhere else the puppy could squeeze behind.

Laundry Room, Mud Room, or Foyer

☐ Detergents, bleach, dryer sheets, and other items are securely stored in cabinets and not on floor.

☐ Coats, shoes, bags, and other sundry items are kept out of puppy's reach.

☐ Doors to the outdoors are always shut. Put a note on the door to remind people to close it firmly.

☐ Keep buckets, mops, and brooms out of the reach of puppy teeth.

Living Room or TV Room

☐ No cords or tassels are dangling from drapes, which the puppy might grab and pull.

☐ Electrical cords are secured or hidden.

☐ Breakable items or valuable items as well as remote controls and candy are removed or placed on high tables or shelves.

☐ Remove area rugs to avoid accidents.

☐ Be wary of toxic house plants.

Bathrooms

- [ ] Keep waste basket, toilet-bowl cleaners, and brush out of puppy's reach.
- [ ] Secure lower cabinets with childproof locks.
- [ ] Keep this room clean so that small items, like dental floss, toothpaste caps, and bandages, aren't eaten by your Rottie.
- [ ] Keep medication, toothpaste, nail clippers, and virtually everything else in this room out of the pup's grasp.
- [ ] Lift up bathroom rugs and mats to avoid puppy accidents and chewing.

Bedrooms

- [ ] Pick up your socks, stockings, slippers, and undergarments: puppies love to chew on (and eat) things that smell like you!
- [ ] Keep chewable containers and hampers in closets; wicker and rubber are canine favorites.
- [ ] Don't let TV wires and cables, cell-phone charger cords, and the like dangle from outlets.
- [ ] Clean out the clutter from under the beds before the puppy gets to it.

Garage and Shed

- [ ] Tidy the garage and shed up to minimize the chance of disaster if the puppy should get into something.
- [ ] Place all fertilizers, antifreeze, windshield-wiper fluid, gas, paint, turpentine, etc., in cabinets out of the pup's reach.
- [ ] Rakes, hoes, shovels, axes, etc., can injure a puppy when he tries to chew on them or steal them.
- [ ] Remove any rodent traps that could snap on your pup's nose or paw and any pesticide strips or containers that your puppy may sample.
- [ ] Don't pile things too high, as they can easily topple over on top of a curious puppy.

Backyard

- [ ] Secure all gaps and holes in the fence to avoid the puppy squeezing out or getting his head stuck; make sure it's 6 feet high so that he doesn't jump over it when he's taller.
- [ ] Scout out toxic plants from your landscape; there are dozens of common plants that can be harmful to dogs.
- [ ] Use mulch that does not contain cocoa hulls.
- [ ] Purchase a lock for the back gate and a sign that says "Beware of Dog."
- [ ] Be wary of the chemicals used on your lawn. Go organic.
- [ ] Wind the hose up so the puppy doesn't claim it as a chew toy.
- [ ] Raise up potted plants to avoid a male puppy watering them unnecessarily.

SOCIALIZE THE PUPPY

In life we've all encountered grown people who simply lack coping mechanisms to deal with problems when they arise. Often the problems that launch these folks into a tail spin are just minor inconveniences, such as a flat tire, the failure of an

Wheel of Misfortune

Car chasing is a very dangerous habit that many dogs engage in. Rottweilers cannot resist the attraction of a moving object, whether it's a bicycle, motorcycle, car, or stroller. Puppies should be socialized to accept objects that roll or else they will grow to chase and attack them. You do not want your Rottweiler chasing a young person on roller skates or jumping into traffic to stop a speeding convertible. Get the puppy accustomed to all of these objects by visiting an outdoor mall or a parking lot, and of course be extremely careful whenever around moving vehicles. Always keep your Rottie on a leash!

appliance repairman to show up on time, or a lost cell phone. Some of these people were raised by doting parents who never set goals for them or expected them to earn their keep. These people usually lack social graces and can be abrupt or inappropriate in social situations.

As annoying and inconsiderate as these folk may be, the dog-world equivalents are much more problematic. Your puppy has to be able to cope with everything that's thrown his way in life—not just a tennis ball or a cheesy treat. *Socialization* is a fancy term that dog behaviorists use to describe "a special learning process during which an individual learns to accept close proximity to various species or to conspecifics of its own group," according to Dr. Bonnie Beaver. In other words, socialization is a time for puppies to get out and meet other dogs. A Rottie who exists only with his family and doesn't see other dogs begins to think he's the only canine left on an island of humans. The term also refers to a period of puppy development in which the puppy begins to bond with his human family. The period extends from the third week to the twelfth and is a critical time to shape the puppy's social behavior. Of course, this nine-week period encompasses many "big" puppy moments:

- The puppy is weaned between weeks four and seven.
- Puppy teeth begin to come in around week three and continue to emerge through week six or eight.
- Playing, barking, and biting begin around five to seven weeks.
- The puppy leaves its dam around eight weeks of age.
- The puppy adjusts to new home environment and humans at eight weeks.
- The puppy loses deciduous teeth between weeks twelve and sixteen.

Puppies need to meet other dogs before they are twelve weeks of age, which means that the first month in your home you have to plan to fill your pup's social calendar with play dates and visits to public places where dogs will be present. Puppies that are not socialized during this critical period often develop behavioral issues which account for four out of five cases of abandoned dogs in the Western world.

Socialization must provide your Rottweiler puppy the opportunity to meet other dogs in a neutral setting as well as to encounter the "unknown." For a puppy, the dark realm of the "unknown" can include scary things like a blender, the warning bell from a dishwasher or washing machine, or a leaf blower. Owners cannot take for granted that the puppy is familiar with the everyday noises in a human environment, and if your puppy was raised in a kennel instead of a kitchen, it's very unlikely he's heard the sounds of a coffee grinder or a microwave oven. Your job as his owner is to show him that these sounds are just ordinary occurrences that don't upset you at all. When the puppy is settling down in the kitchen or bedroom with a

Your puppy's socialization involves his meeting other dogs and people. Once your Rottweiler pup's vaccinations are complete, allow him to meet other dogs and encourage friendly exchanges.

toy, hit the switch on a blender or hairdryer. You can also try this while the puppy is eating his breakfast or dinner. A favorite toy or a bowl of food should be more interesting to the puppy than the clatter of an unknown appliance.

Another source of "strange noises" is emitted from little humans (aka children). If you do not have children in your home, you have to make arrangements to borrow a few for an afternoon, with their parents' permission of course. Invite a friend with dog-savvy children over to your home, or accept an invitation to play at a friend's house or in a public park or playground (in which dogs are allowed). If the puppy is accepting and comfortable with children in a neutral setting, then invite the children to your home so that the puppy realizes that children are fine in his territory too.

Meeting other dogs is key to your puppy's fitting into society: as social animals, dogs are expected to coexist with humans and other dogs (and maybe a cat or two). Dogs naturally live in groups, and unless your puppy was a member of a one-pup litter (very unlikely in a breed like Rottweilers), he spent time with his littermates and learned the canine ropes from his dam and siblings. The breeder should have begun the socialization process before the puppy came home to you, as this is essential to the puppy's not developing a fearful or aggressive response to other dogs or unknown situations.

Many old-time veterinarians and breeders used to recommend that puppies remain isolated from other dogs until their last set of vaccinations was complete. Contemporary thinking has dismissed this, as waiting that long to begin socialization is detrimental to a young puppy. Vets today regard early socialization to be as critical to the development of puppies as worming and inoculations. As long

Choosing a Trainer for Your Rottweiler Puppy

The AKC encourages puppy owners to ask any prospective training instructors a number of questions before signing up for their classes, such as: :

• How long have you been training dogs? How long have you been training puppies?

• What kinds of classes do you teach?

• Have you put any titles on your own dogs? Do you have any certifications as a dog trainer?

• Which dog sports (agility, rally, obedience, etc.) do you participate in or have you participated in?

• What is your basic philosophy of training?

• What kind of equipment (e.g., collars, leashes, etc.) do you use in your classes?

• Do you use food rewards? Corrections? If so, please tell me about these.

• Do puppies of all sizes partiicipate in the same class? Do you have play groups?

• Do you know your drop-out rate? Do many puppies go on to additional training?

as a vaccination protocol has been started, the puppy should be safe to go out and meet other puppies and dogs.

A puppy training class serves many worthwhile purposes for a Rottie owner. In addition to helping the owner bone up on his or her instructor skills and the puppy learn some basic behaviors, it allows the puppy to meet other puppies in a control, safe environment.

The second phase of socialization, which takes us through the eighteenth week, involves taking the puppy out to new places. Bring your puppy to an outdoor mall that welcomes dogs or to a pet-supply super store. At a mall or pet store, the puppy will meet all kinds of people and see a bustling world of people and other dogs. You may also encounter people in wheelchairs or seniors with walkers. Encourage the puppy to say hello to people of all ages, races, sizes, and degrees of mobility.

In order for your Rottweiler puppy to become a normal, happy puppy, you have to commit to his socialization. As J.L. Fuller's classic "K Puppies" experiment from

Consider the Microchip

In addition to using a dog collar and ID tag, think about having your veterinarian insert a microchip in your dog to help find him if he ever gets lost. When scanned, the microchip will show your dog's unique microchip number so that your dog can be returned to you as soon as possible. Go to www.akcreunite.org to learn more about the nonprofit AKC Reunite pet recovery system.

Since 1995, the AKC Reunite service has been selected by millions of dog owners who are grateful for the peace of mind and service that AKC Reunite offers.

the early 1960s illustrated, puppies that are not socialized during the critical first sixteen weeks of life react abnormally to ordinary situations. The twenty puppies in Fuller's experiment withdrew or became immobile when approached or handled by people, could not solve basic problems, and engaged in spoiled-childlike fits. Although in Fuller's day, psychologists didn't use terms like ADHD, many of the puppies in his studies developed into hyperactive, fearful adult dogs with diminished social and learning skills. Although the results of laboratory-type experiments cannot be applied directly to puppies raised in pet homes with regular interaction with people, Fuller's findings confirm that puppies not exposed to humans before the fourteenth week continued to withdraw from human contact and were virtually untrainable.

Puppies need encouragement, lots of praise, and plenty of belly rubs to grow into reliable adult dogs with wonderful personalities.

While no one today doubts the importance of socialization, we also know that exposure to new places and things should not be overdone either. Every puppy is an individual, and owners should make sure not to overexpose the puppy to outside stimuli. In other words, a rowdy St. Patrick's Day parade, a large state fair, or an outlet mall on Black Friday is not recommended! You don't need to seek out construction sites or grammar-school fire drills. Too much too soon can be stressful and scary to a puppy; it's not necessary to expose your puppy to every imaginable situation. Use common sense and always make the puppy feel safe whenever he's encountering new things.

At a Glance ...

Before the puppy comes through the front door, new owners must prepare for the day by shopping for the essential puppy supplies and puppy-proofing their homes and yards.

. . . .

The new owner's shopping list includes: food, bowls, leash, collar, crate, bed, toys, treats, and brushes. You may also want to buy gates to confine the puppy or an ex pen. Cleaning supplies and paper towels are always handy during house-training days.

. . . .

Puppy-proof your home room by room, considering the puppy's safety as well as the possible damage a curious black and tan alligator can do to your things. Don't forget the outdoors, too.

. . . .

The basis for all your Rottweiler's future learning, manners, and life skills lies in how well you socialize him as a puppy. A puppy who is unafraid of strange noises, new places, unknown people and other dogs will grow into a more well-adjusted, biddable adult.

CHAPTER FIVE

The Rottie in Society

Print the letters "CGC" on a Post-it note and place it on your refrigerator or computer screen. Make it an absolute goal to earn the AKC Canine Good Citizen title for your Rottweiler. You will be able to do more than just brag that your dog has an AKC suffix on his name, you'll be assured that you're on the road to having a Rottweiler who will be welcome everywhere he goes.

Rottweiler owners have it tougher than most other dog owners. Rottie people have chosen to take on the greatest dog on the planet, one that is intelligent,

sensitive, and loyal to a fault and one that is powerful, fearless, and strong. It is a huge responsibility to own a dog who will be over 100 pounds of determination and brawn.

Begin your stewardship of the Rottweiler by learning as much as possible about how to raise and train this extraordinary breed of dog. You have to know how to become a better dog owner, more responsible, more knowledgeable and smarter than owners of "ordinary" dogs. Rottie owners have a higher duty, and the future of the breed depends upon it.

Much of your success with your Rottweiler depends on your commitment to socialize the puppy and your ability to train the dog to understand right from wrong. Humans and dogs don't see eye to snout on most matters of right and wrong, so our goal as trainers is to convince the puppy to see things our way. While your eight-week-old puppy is still small enough for you to pick him up and actually talk to him face to face, take advantage of this while you can. "Listen, little guy: your dad's got this, now settle down." A puppy needs to recognize and respect your authority. He will understand better when you can physically pick him and remove him from a situation. That little guy is going to grow before your very eyes: a two-month-old Rottweiler puppy (usually about 18 to 25 pounds) will gain an average of 10 pounds a month for the next six months; at nine months of age (85 to 95 pounds), the puppy's weight gain usually slows down.

Make sure your puppy's collar fits him properly. Check the tightness daily and adjust it if you cannot fit two sideways fingers underneath it.

LEASH TRAINING

A walk around the block with your Rottie should be an enjoyable, rejuvenating activity. An owner should look forward to quality time spent with a dog when he or she can relax and breathe in the surroundings. Of course, this perfect bonding experience is only possible if the owner has invested the time into leash training the puppy before he grows into a 100-pound tugging machine. Unless you are 200 pounds of muscle yourself, there is no way to walk an untrained adult Rottweiler, so begin leash training when you can still control your dog.

Your successful relationship with your Rottweiler puppy must be built on trust, love, and discipline, and walking lessons reinforce all of these. Your puppy must understand from the onset that you are the one in charge of the leash. Begin with your puppy on your left side and the leash in your right hand. By allowing the leash to hang across your body, you're avoiding slack in the leash, and using the opposite hand to hold the leash discourages you from holding it too tightly. Before you start, make sure you have the puppy's attention. When he's looking at you, say "Let's go," using a happy, animated voice, and start walking forward slowly.

Once the puppy starts moving, encourage him by saying "Good, puppy, let's go." Some distracted puppies refuse to give you their full attention and may need more than verbal praise. Choose a tasty food treat and let your puppy sniff it so that he knows that you have it in your hand. He doesn't need to taste it: it's enough encouragement for him to know there's liver close by. With the puppy in his starting position, reach down with your food treat and let him smell it, and then begin moving forward.

Community Involvement

Have you seen a bumper sticker that says, "I own a Rottweiler and I vote!"? Responsible dog owners, and Rottie owners in particular, need to make their presence known in their communities. These versatile working dogs have so much to offer humankind as police dogs, service dogs, search and rescue dogs, and therapy dogs, and owners must help keep all of these positive images fresh in the public's mind.

Begin by entering your Rottweiler in a training class and attaining the AKC Canine Good Citizen award. Pursue further training in obedience and participate in obedience trials, or possibly agility, rally or tracking, with your Rottie. Work toward having your dog certified as a therapy dog so that you can visit local nursing homes and hospitals. Join a local dog training club, tracking club, or breed club. Sign up your Rottie to participate in a charity walk or a local parade for Oktoberfest!

If your Rottie puppy is being stubborn and testing you, ignore him and keep walking. "Let's go" and a little tug tell him that you're the one deciding the direction and the speed of the walk. If the puppy plops down (and you know that he's not overly tired or hot), crouch down in front of him and say "Come here, baby boy (or girl)." As the puppy gets up and comes to you, turn and start moving on your walk. Keep the distance short. It's better to go back and forth over the same area than to venture a few blocks from home. Once the puppy is walking consistently, start working on about turns and right and left turns. As you add these turns to your puppy's repertory, he begins to understand that he has to pay attention to know which way you're headed.

Walking on a leash will be an exciting activity for your puppy. Next to meal times, a walk with his owner will become his favorite time of day. While stubborn puppies may refuse to walk with you, more likely than not your puppy will try to jet forward ahead of you so that he can discover what new scents and sights await the two of you. When your puppy pulls on the leash, you have to stop in your tracks and not move forward. The puppy needs to learn to walk at your pace, and that pace should not be hurried. Young pups can strain their growing legs by running too fast or haphazardly.

Rottweilers need owners who "get it." A breed as intelligent, powerful, and commanding of respect as the Rottweiler requires a special person in his life.

POSITIVE TRAINING

Two great positive-training techniques are lure-reward training and clicker training. Lure-reward training is based on enticing the dog to obey through a food treat and verbal praise. Clicker training or marker training involves using a clicker to "mark" the desired behavior the precise moment it occurs. After the trainer clicks, he can give the dog a food reward.

The concept of negative punishment will be familiar to parents who for generations have been sending their kids to their rooms for misbehaving. In this training approach, the

Puppy Exercise

Your Rottweiler puppy will set the pace and tone of his needed exercise. Since Rottie pups are heavy for their size, their little frames are carrying a bulky load. During the first year, a pup's bones and joints are not fully developed. Don't overdo exercise with a puppy, and avoid jumping games or other strenuous activities. Rottweiler puppies don't play gently, so be careful when your puppy is playing with older, larger dogs who can easily injure your puppy.

owner deprives the dog of something desirable. It could be withdrawing a food treat, ending a game of catch, or simply ignoring the dog, all of which serve to remove something positive from the dog's environment.

Avoid trainers who use harsh methods, especially what trainers call "positive punishment" that uses pinch or electric collars, harsh vocal corrections, citronella sprays, or the like. Despite its name, "negative reinforcement" works much better: turning your back and ignoring your dog when he jumps on you is the "negative" that the dog wants to see removed. Only when the dog stops jumping is the negative element removed from his environment. Likewise, refusing to walk when the puppy is pulling on the leash is another form of negative reinforcement.

SOLVING PUPPY PROBLEMS

Rottie puppies are easily excited, and when a puppy is excited he wants to play...and nip and mouth and chew. If yours is a chaos-filled home, with lots of noise, children running in and out, or teenagers keeping crazy hours, your puppy is going to react accordingly. Minimizing the noise and activity helps to establish a more stable learning environment for your Rottweiler puppy.

Teach the Rottweiler puppy that he has to earn what he wants in life: there are no free rides, lunches, or rawhide strips. Owners structure their dogs' meals, walks, play times, and naps; and everything has a price. In order to get his dinner bowl or to go for a walk, the puppy must sit and stay; the puppy must not pull on the leash in order to move forward; the dog must be quiet to get a treat.

Whenever you're playing with the puppy, keep a leash on him, which can act as a handle to help you control the puppy when he starts to misbehave. If you have to use the leash to correct the puppy, make sure you do so swiftly and purposefully. Make the puppy know that you mean business, otherwise he will continue to carry on assuming that you're playing a game.

Most Rottweiler puppies are bursting with energy and want to have things their way. They dart out in front of you when you open a door; they jump up on visitors and furniture; they pull on their leashes like a pack of Huskies on a race; they bark and dig; they steal food and grab clothing. The prospect of dealing with all of these nuisance behaviors could persuade any potential dog owner to consider a different breed or species. However, an owner who understands why his or her Rottweiler does the things he does has the needed advantage to prevent or fix any of these issues.

Nipping problems in the bud or preventing them entirely is much easier than solving problems further down the road. Preventive measures pay off. While all puppies exhibit nuisance behaviors like barking, begging, and stealing food, we will begin with the most important lesson: bite inhibition or discouraging and stopping mouthing, nipping, and biting.

Bite Inhibition

When you're first sitting and playing with your puppy, inevitably he will try to use your fingers or hands as a chew toy. There is a difference between nipping and mouthing. Mouthing is not painful, and canines use it to get your attention or tell you they want something, such as more petting or a second cookie. A puppy mouthing your hand and fingers can be used to teach the puppy what is acceptable and what

is not. Your Rottie puppy needs to understand that human hands and skin are very fragile and that he must respect them.

Baby puppies learn the limits of behavior from their siblings, and when play got too rough or bites got too hard, yelping and crying ended the game. Once the puppy learns sufficient bite inhibition, he uses a softer, gentler mouth in play. When the pup attempts to chomp down on your fingers with his needle-sharp teeth, your reaction should be to yelp in pain, swiftly pull away your hand, and make a terrible fuss. Over-reacting tells the puppy that you are hurt and upset by his behavior. Repeat this as many times as necessary. If you have to turn your back on your puppy and ignore him for a few minutes, he will get that message too. Rotties *hate* to be ignored, especially by their favorite human playmate.

As the puppy is learning to bite softer on your hand, tolerate less and less pressure by saying "Ouch" sooner. Little by little, you are teaching the puppy the importance of an inhibited bite, but time is not on your side. Those tiny jaws and prickly teeth of the puppy will soon develop into the powerful jaws and punishing teeth of an adult Rottweiler. You have to make the dog comprehend this lesson before his strength increases.

If after a few weeks you're not seeing any progress, then your bull-headed puppy is all Rottweiler and will require you to take a more serious approach. Learn to use your voice and body language to convey to the puppy that you are absolutely serious about bite inhibition. Many dog owners are guilty of being charmed by their cute puppies' bad habits. YouTube is brimming with naughty puppies, and who can resist laughing when a baby Rottweiler barks "aggressively" at the old family cat or softly growls at Aunt Mona? Owners inadvertently encourage unwanted behavior by laughing and clapping, and most Rottweilers enjoy being the center of attention, whether it's as the class bully or the class clown.

Communicate your likes and dislikes to your Rottweiler. A well-behaved Rottie will want nothing more than to please you.

Be Proactive!

If your puppy is continuing to nip at you or other family members or friends, then a more serious aggression problem can be developing. Be proactive before this type behavior escalates and consider what factors may be aggravating the behavior in the dog's environment. Do not engage in tug of war games or physical challenges with the puppy. Do not tease the puppy with a toy as games like this can motivate the dog to clamp down on an object to hold it still or win it for himself. If the situation continues to deteriorate, seek professional assistance immediately.

A word about growling: No puppy growls at his human unless he's distressed. Growling is a dog's first warning sign: it says, "whatever you're doing to me, I don't like it, and I really would prefer you to stop." A dog in distress will stare directly at you, show his teeth, snarl, and maybe even snap at the air. He is giving a warning sign that he may bite. Heed the puppy's warning, and focus on what is causing the distress.

Like mouthing, nipping can also indicate that the puppy wants something. If the puppy is restless, chewing on your hands may be his way of relieving his anxiety or boredom. The more excited the puppy is, the harder he will bite in play. Consider taking the puppy out for a play session in the yard or for a short walk around the block. You can also place a chew toy in the puppy's mouth so that he gets the idea that your hand is not made out of rawhide and is less fun to chew on. Praise him for using the chew toy.

Never resort to hitting your puppy or spraying foul-tasting stuff in his face or mouth. Rottweilers are very sensitive and you should reserve discipline for extreme situations. Never correct your puppy with anger. Corrections for a puppy should never be physical, as rough-handling, such as shaking, grabbing, or forcing the dog into a down position, will only serve to scare the puppy. When a dog experiences fear, his natural reaction is to protect himself (which means bite). A dog's teeth are his only weapon. If a dog thinks his life is in danger, he will either fight back or flee. Engaging in physical corrections does not earn the dog's trust and respect, instead it tells him that you are an enemy to be avoided. No creature wants to be bossed around by a fearmonger.

Make Your Puppy a S.T.A.R.

The American Kennel Club has a great program for new puppy owners called the S.T.A.R. Puppy® Program, which is dedicated to rewarding puppies that get off to a good start by completing a basic training class. S.T.A.R. stands for Socialization, Training, Activity, and Responsibility.

You must enroll in a six-week puppy-training course with an AKC-approved evaluator. When the class is finished, the evaluator will test your puppy on all of the training taught during the course, such as being free of aggression toward people and other puppies in the class, tolerating a collar or body harness, allowing his owner to take away a treat or toy, and sitting and coming on command.

If your puppy passes the test, he will receive a certificate and a medal. You and your puppy will also be listed in the AKC S.T.A.R. Puppy records. To learn more about the AKC S.T.A.R. Puppy Program or to find an approved evaluator, check out www.akc.org/puppies/training/index.cfm.

Barking

Too often trainers blame everything on the Rottweiler's desire to be dominant over people and other dogs. While no one will argue that the Rottweiler can be the domineering type, he's not barking at you or people on the street to tell them that he wants to be the boss. There can be a hundred reasons why a Rottie will bark at his owner or family, and they range from sheer boredom and separation anxiety to his dislike of something in his environment or his fear that someone or something is threatening his turf. A Rottweiler is doing his job by barking at a stranger on the street or at someone approaching the front door or gate. An owner should learn to ignore the Rottweiler's barking when it is purposeless and only pay attention and praise the dog when he's protecting the home or warning you of an actual threat. By scolding the dog (barking at him) and giving him attention when he barks for no reason, you are inadvertently reinforcing the behavior.

By no means should you use a treat to quiet your Rottweiler. If the Rottie barks and you say "Quiet" and give him a treat, he believes that the bark earned him a treat. Give the "Quiet" cue and let him settle down, after a minute of silence, give him a treat (for being quiet).

Jumping Up

Jumping up is problem that must be resolved while the puppy is still young and not able to topple a grown man. Dogs don't jump up for any reason other than to greet you: it's not a matter of domination or a way to assert their rank. When the puppy attempts to jump up, place your hands on his shoulders and return his four feet to the floor. Squat down and greet the puppy at his level. Your Rottweiler should be trained to sit and stay whenever people return home or visitors arrive. Make sure all family members insist that the puppy is sitting before they acknowledge the puppy. If the puppy continues to jump up, turn your back on him and ignore him. If you greet the puppy while he's jumping up on you, you're only reinforcing the unwanted behavior. Be sure that everyone in your household is following the same protocol to prevent jumping in the future.

Did You Know?

The Rottweiler was originally devised as a dog who could move cattle, and there's no doubt that herding cattle is difficult, challenging work for dog and human. A droving dog often would have to work far away from his master and be able to make decisions for himself. Rotties today are self-motivated, free-thinking canines that require a confident owner to train.

Never tease your Rottweiler. Instead, engage him in fun, productive games and teach him to obey commands in a variety of settings.

Possessiveness

Sharing doesn't come natural to dogs, though it's not impossible to teach your Rottweiler to become trusting enough to share his possessions, including his toys, food bowl, and favorite bone. Dr. Ian Dunbar, one of the pioneers of positive training, says that "Feelings of possessiveness and protectiveness basically stem from insecurity, lack of trust and lack of socialization: it takes confidence to share." The process of teaching dogs to share relies upon increasing their enjoyment of having humans around their treasured stuff. A dog who respects your authority should not fuss if you grab his bowl or rubber bone.

A good preventive measure for food-bowl possessiveness is to sit on the floor next to your puppy while he's eating. By walking away after placing the bowl on the floor, the puppy gets the message that he eats alone and that's the way it's supposed to be. It's better to talk to him and bond with him while he's eating, without interrupting him, so that he feels secure with you nearby. You can also add a couple pieces of chicken or cheese to his bowl while he's eating so that he thinks it's a good thing any time you touch his bowl. You can also considering hand-feeding the dog the first half of his meal or offering him a treat while he's eating from the bowl.

If your Rottie has already developed food-bowl possessiveness, then let's try what Dr. Dunbar calls the "delinquent waiter" routine. It goes something like this: Prepare your dog's food in his bowl while he's on the floor ready to eat. When it's ready, place an empty bowl on the floor and watch him approach it. He will sniff and look up at you pathetically as if you're the worst waiter he's ever seen. After ten or twenty seconds, walk over to the bowl with two pieces of kibble and drop them into the bowl. After he gulps those two tidbits, he will look at you again and may even bark to let you know that he knows you're messing with him (and that you're not getting a tip!). Repeat the same process again, perhaps with four pieces of kibble, and so forth until he's allowed you near his bowl five or six times. Now pick up the bowl and fill it halfway. Holding the bowl in your left hand, offer the dog a tasty treat with your right, and a then a few more.

You'll have to repeat this game a few days in a row, and once the dog accepts your presence around his bowl, it's time to interrupt his eating by coming to him with a tasty treat. Hold the treat far enough away so that you can take hold of his bowl with your other hand. Repeat this a few times so that he doesn't feel threatened by your touching his bowl. You can also take the bowl away for a moment or two and place something delicious in it so that the dog realizes that his owner isn't going to steal his food, he's going to improve it.

Possessiveness over toys can be overcome in a few stages. First, determine which toys your dog loves and which ones aren't favorites. Begin with a toy that the dog is lukewarm about. Once he reluctantly takes it from you, propose a trade: this tasty treat for that so-so toy. The dog will always take the treat. Progress to toys that the dog likes more and upgrade the quality of your treats. When you get to the most favorite toy, you' may have to bribe him with half a hot dog, a hunk of filet, or fresh tuna. No Rottie can resist a truly delectable treat, and you are augmenting the dog's trust of you around his favorite things.

A Rottie with his favorite Toys! This quintet of Chihuahuas feels perfectly safe in the capable paws of their black and tan housemate.

At a Glance ...

Walking a trained, mannerly Rottweiler will be a daily pleasure for you. Begin training the puppy right away so that he learns to walk on a loose leash without pulling ahead or tugging.

. . . .

Positive-training methods, using rewards and possibly a clicker, are the best ways to train the sensitive and sometimes stubborn Rottweiler. Harsh methods and punishment can quickly ruin a Rottie.

. . . .

Be proactive in redirecting your puppy's behavior and avoiding potential bad habits from forming. Bite-inhibition training must be on the top of every new Rottweiler owner's list. Owners must also nip barking, jumping, and possessive behaviors in the bud, too.

CHAPTER SIX

House-Training Your Rottweiler

The urgent need to house-train your new Rottweiler puppy becomes apparent the first time he pees on your kitchen floor or carpet. There's a moment of slight panic as the new owner realizes the he or she is living with a new "clear and present danger": a messy, smelly house.

While most owners can deal with a dog who doesn't always sit on command or who pulls occasionally on a walk, no owner can weather a dog who relieves himself randomly around the

house. House-training is the owner's most pressing goal, and you have to be ready to tackle it.

The tools that you'll need are patience, consistency, and a crate. A roll of paper towels and an odor-neutralizer are also handy. Let's talk about that scary little five-letter word: C-R-A-T-E.

GOD MADE CRATES

Ever since cavemen and caveladies opened their caves to friendly, hungry wolf pups, humans have regarded dogs as companions. Thousands of years later, we view dogs as members of our family. You often hear people refer to themselves as dog parents and not just owners. (For legal purposes, however, you are your dog's owner not his parent.) As a loving owner, it's natural that you will want to spare your puppy from harsh treatment and negative experiences, and you think that might include locking your puppy up in a metal cage. If you think that using a dog crate is a mean, drastic measure employed by inattentive, heartless owners, you're not alone. Many ill-informed, inexperienced new dog owners think the same thing.

Luckily, your Rottweiler doesn't think that way at all. The concept of crate training stems from those wolf pups' instinct to live in a den. Wolves would burrow in the ground or find a crevice to sleep and retreat from the worries of the woods. Your puppy seeks the same kind of protection, and the crate satisfies his desire for a den.

As a safe haven for your puppy, the crate is also hallowed ground: an area where the dog does not urinate or defecate. Mama wolf, who for thousands of years never changed a diaper, wisely taught her pups, never poop where you sleep. Or piddle. Therein lies the blessing of a dog crate. Your Rottweiler puppy will regard his dog crate as a sanctuary all his own, and he will look forward to his "lone wolf" hours napping, chewing on a bone, or just daydreaming about his next romp around the block.

Your Rottweiler will continue to use his crate when he's an adult, so it's sensible to purchase a large crate so that you don't have to replace a smaller one when the puppy outgrows it. The crate you'll need for an adult Rottie is 48 inches long and 36 inches wide. For the puppy, you can section off half the crate so that he doesn't relieve himself on one end and sleep on the other. To section off the crate, use a piece of Plexiglas, Masonite, or any polycarbonate polymer board that you can find cheaply. Make sure it's safely positioned so that it won't fall in on the puppy and be sure that he cannot chew it.

Most Rottweilers are fairly easy to house-train. They grasp the concept naturally and take to their crates without fuss. It requires little preparation to introduce the puppy to his crate. You want to situate the crate in an area of the house where the family gathers, either the kitchen or a family or TV room. Leave the crate door open and let the puppy explore it on his own. Place a towel or a washable crate mat on the bottom of the crate. The more comfortable it is, the more likely the puppy is to settle in. Once the puppy walks into the crate (or better yet, lies down), offer him a favorite toy. Tell him he's good, and pet him. Give him a couple more treats.

If the puppy ignores the crate entirely, you can lure him into the crate with a handful of treats. Toss one into the crate and encourage him to get it. Once he's inside, give him a couple more. Work on this before dinner, so that he's hungry. If he

Extra! Extra!

The old conventional training method of using newspaper is not advised for the Rottweiler. While owners of smaller dogs, particular those who live in the city, still paper-train their dogs, this transitional step doesn't work with a dog the size of a Rottweiler. You're better off using the crate and getting the puppy outside swiftly.

ignores the treat, you may have to come up with more enticing tidbits, like a piece of cheese or chicken.

If you've followed the advice in the previous chapters, you've likely purchased your puppy from a reputable breeder. Another advantage of purchasing from a good Rottweiler breeder is that he or she probably already started your puppy's crate training, which is the preferred house-training method of most breeders. If you're lucky, the breeder introduced the puppies to crates when they were five or six weeks of age, allowing them to sleep in pairs in a crate and eventually individually. Be sure to thank your breeder for giving you a head start!

THE DAILY ROUTINE

If the puppy was raised in the breeder's home, that's another great advantage when it comes to house-training. Even though your home will look and smell different than the breeder's house, at the very least the puppy is familiar with various surfaces (tiles, carpet, hardwood, linoleum, etc.) and has likely been cordoned into certain areas of the breeder's home.

You have to limit your puppy's exploration of your home during the first week. This is when those baby gates come in handy. Limit the puppy to one or two rooms, ideally ones without carpeting and definitely one that has access to the outside. You want the puppy to know where the "potty exit" is so that he can head toward it when he has to go.

Experienced breeders introduce their pups to crates before leaving for their new homes. If you're lucky enough to have acquired your puppy from such a breeder, you're a few steps ahead in the house-training game.

A Tot That Trots

Slow down there! Follow your puppy's lead. When you take your Rottie puppy out for a walk, allow him to go at his own tempo instead of trying to hurry him along to walk at your speed. His legs are much shorter than yours, and puppies don't need to learn to trot too early. When puppies are tired, they will plop down to rest, so allow your pup to stop when he wants to. You may stress his growing bones by trying to make him walk farther and faster than he wants to.

Owners have to be on red alert when watching young puppies in the house. *Yellow alert* is actually the more appropriate name for this watch, and you have to know the signs of a puppy getting ready to go.

- sniffing at the floor in an urgent fashion
- whining or whimpering
- turning in a circle
- pacing
- restlessness
- moving quickly to another area
- standing by the "potty exit"

If your puppy knows where the exit is, and he's standing there or circling, you have exactly five seconds to get him outside. Young puppies do not give you much warning sign before they squat: when they have to go, they usually have to go *now*. Like human babies, puppies have no bladder or bowel control. The owner must be always ready to pick up the puppy and get him to his outdoor potty spot. Accidents occur when the owner is distracted by other things or when the owner simply isn't paying attention to the puppy's signs. As the puppy gets older, he will give clearer signs and be able to hold it long enough to get outside.

When you take the puppy outside, you want to bring him to the same spot every time. He will recognize his scent in the grass or whatever surface you choose, and he will use it again. It's best not to choose a hard surface like cement or asphalt. The puppy will welcome a softer, more comfy terrain...something as comfortable as the carpet in the family room, for instance.

Whenever your puppy relieves himself in the designated area, praise him lavishly and give him a treat. Don't get in the habit of giving the dog a treat for coming back inside. The treat is for the desired behavior of relieving himself *outside* (which means you have to be out there with him to reward him). Smart Rotties will come running back to the door to get their treat and not give a second thought to taking care of their business.

Limit Crate Time

How long can you confine your puppy to this crate? At eight to ten weeks of age, a puppy's limit would be about 60 to 90 minutes. An eleven- to fourteen-week old puppy can last about two to three hours in his crate. Four hours is the limit for a puppy six months of age or older. Adolescents whose bones, muscles, and ligaments are still growing shouldn't be confined for longer periods, as they need to stretch their limbs and exercise. Adults shouldn't be left in their crates for more than four or five hours at a time. Once the dog is house-trained fully, the crate serves as a refuge and the door should remain open. Your Rottweiler can't protect your home from the other side of a locked crate door.

Getting your Rottweiler puppy on a schedule is critical to house-training success. Setting times for meals, exercise, and naps will provide structure to your puppy's day and give you an advantage for predicting relief patterns. Take your puppy outside:

- when he wakes up from a nap
- when he's been released from his crate
- fifteen minutes after he finishes eating
- five minutes after he's taken a drink
- right after he's run around the room a dozen times
- after he's become excited from visitors or someone returning home

The puppy will need to be taken outside to relieve himself about ten to twenty times a day until he's four or five months of age.

Grass is every puppy's favorite backdrop He can relax in it, roll in it, eat it, and pee in it, and all he gets is satisfaction and praise!

A PIECE OF HISTORY

The first Rottweiler to work as a police dog in Germany was reportedly Flock von Hamburg who worked for the Hamburg Police Force. On the force, Flock and Max von der Stahlenberg were promoted by an Inspector Hinsch, and the breed was recognized as an official police dog in Germany.

Can Your Dog Pass the Canine Good Citizen® Test?

Once your Rottweiler is ready for advanced training, you can start training him for the American Kennel Club Canine Good Citizen® Program. This program is for dogs that are trained to behave at home, out in the neighborhood, and in the city. It's easy and fun to do. Once your dog learns basic obedience and good canine manners, a CGC evaluator gives your dog ten basic tests. If he passes, he's awarded a Canine Good Citizen® certificate. Many trainers offer classes, and the test is the "final exam" to graduate. To find an evaluator in your area, go to www.akc.org/events/cgc/cgc_bystate.cfm.

Many therapy dogs and guide dogs are required to pass the Canine Good Citizen® test in order to help as working and service dogs in the community. There are ten specific skills that a dog must master in order to pass the Canine Good Citizen® test:

1. **Let a friendly stranger approach and talk to his owner**
2. **Let a friendly stranger pet him**
3. **Be comfortable being groomed and examined by a friendly stranger**
4. **Walk on a leash and show that he is under control and not overly excited**
5. **Move through a crowd politely and confidently**
6. **Sit and stay on command**
7. **Come when called**
8. **Behave calmly around another dog**
9. **Not bark at or react to a surprise distraction**
10. **Show that he can be left with a trusted person away from his owner**

In order to help your dog pass the AKC CGC test, first enroll him in basic training classes or a CGC training class. You can find classes and trainers near you by searching the AKC website. When you feel that your dog is ready to take the test, locate an AKC-approved CGC evaluator to set up a test date, or sign up for a test that is held at a local AKC dog show or training class. For more information about the AKC Canine Good Citizen® Program, visit www.akc.org/events.cgc.

"Go to Your Room!"

Parents still send their misbehaving children (and teenagers?) to their rooms, and you may be tempted to shut your naughty puppy in his crate and say "Bad dog." Don't. Your puppy has to maintain a positive association with his crate, so never bring him to his crate when you're angry or frustrated with his behavior. Take a minute to breathe, grab a treat, and happily lead the offender to his crate.

SPEED THE PUP

There is no hard and fast rule about how long it takes to house-train a puppy. Some puppies learn much faster than others and can be fairly reliable indoors in four to six weeks, others can take a whole year to house-train.

It is certainly easier to house-train a puppy during the warmer months of the year. Though Rottweilers are fairly tolerant of cold weather, they would rather go outside in the spring and fall. Rainy weather is not a favorite of the Rottweiler, and potty trips have to happen every day, whether it's raining, snowing, or blowing! You'll have to rough it right alongside your Rottie puppy. If you let your puppy into the backyard alone, he may simply hang out under the awning or sit next to the back door and not do his business.

A puppy can be trained to relieve himself on concrete or gravel, though neither is as fun (or easy) as grass.

Ten Secrets of House-Training

1. Feed your puppy at scheduled intervals and don't overdo treats.

2. Offer the puppy water at set times throughout the day. Free access to a water bowl all day means the puppy will piddle on and off all day.

3. Limit the puppy's water intake in the evening, as well as before and after meals.

4. Take the puppy out to the same spot outdoors every time. He will recognize his scent and use it again.

5. Use the same door to take your puppy outside. He will go to that door when he knows he has to go.

6. Don't be nonchalant when your puppy relieves himself outdoors—let him see you celebrate.

7. Never correct the puppy for mistakes—simply be more watchful.

8. Clean up accidents in the house with a pet-odor neutralizer not just soap and water (and never ammonia). The dog's nose will find the spot and repeat the mistake.

9. Puppies need to eliminate 15 to 30 minutes after they eat a meal. Don't delay.

10. Use the crate whenever you cannot be actively watching the puppy.

You can do your part to expedite the process by being as consistent and attentive as humanly possible. It is not realistic to think that you can watch the puppy 24/7, which is when the crate comes in handy. If you have to run an errand or are going to be in a different area of the house doing chores or getting ready for work, put the puppy in the crate with a toy and do what you have to do.

Don't let puppy mishaps dishearten you. Accidents in the house can be frustrating, especially once you think your puppy is "nearly there." Relapses in house-training are very common, though they occur for various reasons. A puppy could contract a urinary tract infection or his hormones could be raging and he's marking in the house. Retrace your steps and rule out a medical issue before attempting to identify a behavioral cause. Dominance marking is common in male puppies, though a puppy could develop a submissive urination behavior during his second fear period (four to six months of age).

Another snare to speedy house-training success may have to do with how you're cleaning up after those accidents. A Rottweiler's nose is capable of detecting a drop of blood in a

Most Rottie pups learn house-training with little effort. If your puppy is taking a bit longer, be patient and make sure you're being consistent. The puppy can't house-train himself!

thousand gallons of water. If the puppy can still smell his urine on the floor, he will naturally revisit the spot. You have to thoroughly clean the spot and neutralize the odor. White vinegar and water is the most affordable way to remove the smell of urine. Use one part white vinegar to three parts warm water. Allow the area to soak for seven or eight minutes, and then clean up with a mild soap. Pet shops sell terrific solutions to remove pet odors, and many owners believe they are worth the investment.

At a Glance ...

Based on the mindset of den-dwelling wolves, crate training is the easiest way to train a dog not to mess in the house. It is critical for owners to learn the proper way to use a dog crate.

· ·

Rottweilers are intelligent dogs who respond to crate training with ease, as long as owners maintain a regimented schedule during the process.

· ·

Limit the puppy's access to only a couple of rooms in the house. Teach the puppy to use the same door to go outside and the same area in the yard to relieve himself.

· ·

Thoroughly clean up potty-training accidents in the house: your Rottie's nose will easily locate the site of his last piddle and he will likely repeat his offense.

CHAPTER SEVEN

Rottweiler U

Your Rottweiler can become a straight-A student, but you need to know what it takes to become his favorite professor. "Dogs in general seem to be a very pragmatic lot and the Rottweiler in particular exemplifies this, sometimes to the extreme. They tend to do what brings them pleasure and avoid what brings them displeasure. However, a good handler will recognize that this trait can be made an asset rather than a liability, for the Rottweiler's reticence to do what bores him is surpassed only by his boundless enthusiasm for doing what he enjoys."

9/11 Search Dog

Rottweiler "Phoenix," a certified cadaver search dog, was one of the canine heroes of September 11th who worked in the recovery mission at the Fresh Kills Landfill, where the rubble from the Twin Towers was hauled. Phoenix and her handler Denise Grimm, members of the New Jersey Rescue and Recovery K-9 Unit, located numerous body parts that brought closure to the victims' families. Grimm described her search partner as "a role model for the Rottweiler breed [who] set a high standard at Fresh Kills [and] worked long hours with few breaks, never faltering in her desire to 'find'." Phoenix is featured in the award-winning book *Dog Heroes of September 11th: A Tribute to America's Search and Rescue Dogs* by Nona Kilgore Bauer (i5 Press, 2011).

Those words come to us from George L. Beck, the owner and trainer of OTCH Mondberg's Donnamire V Beier, the breed's first Obedience Trial Champion, and they describe an intelligent dog who naturally responds to *positive reinforcement*. As B. F. Skinner and the behaviorists who followed him describe this concept: positive reinforcement means that any behavior that is rewarded is repeated. The Rottweiler is a super smart, sensitive animal that does not respond well to harsh treatment or punishment.

Positive training does not mean that every lesson is going to be a smorgasbord of liver cookies and bacon bits; in fact, using treats while training the dog indicates to the dog that you are the source of things that he wants. And as the controller of the liver and bacon, you can also withhold the very things he wants. He learns to please

Whether a young puppy or a mature adult, the Rottweiler is a sensitive dog that responds best to positive-traning methods.

you to earn the things that you control. That's a fancy way of explaining that food is a great motivator for dogs, just as ice cream and pizza are great motivators for children.

Treats aren't useful only during training sessions: you should have a supply of them with you all day long. Let your puppy believe that you can magically make a treat appear whenever he does something good—no matter where you are or what time of day. In order to sustain the magical illusion, don't let your puppy see the bag of treats. When the puppy hears the bag crinkling, he switches gears and will automatically sit or pay attention. Obedience isn't reserved for lesson time: you want your puppy to be attentive to you all of the time. He knows that a good leader is on duty 24/7.

Canines look for someone to point the way; however, in the absence of a credible top dog, the Rottweiler will try to assume control. When your pup was living with his dam—just a few short weeks ago—she demonstrated to him that she was "the bitch in charge." Not only did she provide food and affection, but she was a lot bigger and knew when to raise one of her big bear paws to correct him. A Rottie puppy being cuffed by his dam knows he's doing something wrong. Rottweilers respect power and authority. Essentially you are assuming the dam's role and you have to make sure that your puppy knows that you are to be respected at all times. This doesn't require that you raise a paw to your puppy, the way his mom did, but rather that you communicate your desires to him clearly so that he grasps what it is you want.

Puppy training is not a project that you can start next week. Many owners make the mistake of putting off lessons so they can spend time bonding and playing with their irresistible, roly-poly Rottie toddlers. You have to do both: puppy school includes both lessons and recess, so there's plenty of time for fun and games as well as socialization and basic obedience lessons. The puppy's biological clock is ticking, and he is most moldable before he reaches twenty weeks of age, which means that you have twelve weeks to teach your puppy his manners and lessons and to make him feel like a valuable, loved member of your family.

With a student as intelligent as the Rottweiler, you run the risk of boring your dog with too much repetition. The Rottie will not sit fourteen times in a row: by the fourth or fifth time, he will give you the look that says, "I got this...what else you want?" Your challenge as your Rottweiler's trainer is to keep lessons interesting and fun for the dog.

DOG-FRIENDLY TRAINER

If you are considering bringing your puppy to a private instructor, make sure you find one who is using "dog-friendly" methods. Reward-based positive training is the best method for training a Rottweiler. Harsh correction-based training is the wrong way to go with this sensitive breed. The first clue that the trainer is heavy-handed will be the kinds of collars that he or she recommends: chain choke collars, prong collars, and electric shock collars are definite bad signs. Too many trainers think that large, powerful dogs like Rottweilers require tougher, forceful handling to train and control. Avoid trainers who practice dominance tactics, and if you're not completely comfortable with the instructor, seek out the right one. There are hundreds of dog trainers out there, and with some research you can find the right one for your puppy.

Did You Know?

The hit HBO series *Entourage*, which began in 2004, featured a Rottweiler named Arnold (portrayed by canine actor, Rocky). In the show, Arnold belongs to Salvatore "Turtle" Vacara (actor Jerry Ferrara), and he arrived in the first episode in a dog crate and stayed on the series for all eight seasons. In one episode, Turtle's buddy, Johnny "Drama" Chase (actor Kevin Dillon) uses Arnold's friendly disposition to flirt with ladies in the dog park. Here's his ode to the breed: "True dog people know that a Rott's tough exterior is merely a protective shell that hides a wealth of sensitivity they have within."

Eye Contact

Depending on whom you ask, you will get widely divergent answers on the question of whether or not to make direct eye contact with a Rottweiler. Some trainers say *never* stare at a Rottweiler either because it enrages them or challenges them. When a Rottweiler looks into your eyes, you do not have to worry that you're giving in to him or making him feel superior. In your eyes, your dog should see leadership and confidence not anger or antagonism. Direct eye contact is necessary when training a dog, and you'll never maintain the attention of a dog who is diverting your gaze.

Set aside two times each day to train your puppy, perhaps in the morning and late afternoon. Your own schedule will dictate when will work best for you, but just be sure that lesson times are *before* meal times and *after* a good walk or play session. Hungry, well-exercised dogs make better students. A puppy who's been shut away indoors all day, or just released from his crate, will be brimming with energy and will not be able to settle down for a lesson. Choose a quiet area of your house where you know your puppy won't be distracted. Concentrate on one lesson, such as sit or stay, and practice it in the same place every day. Once the puppy grasps the lesson, take him outside and try it in the yard (or another room of the house). The yard naturally will present more distractions to your puppy, so you may have to work harder and offer an extra treat to entice the puppy to repeat a behavior.

A puppy lesson should last no more than ten minutes. That may sound like nothing, but you will soon discover that keeping a puppy focused for ten minutes *in a row* is actually a challenge. If your puppy's attention starts to lag or he shows signs of stress or boredom, vary the cues or exercises or simply resume training later. You don't want the puppy to think of his lesson times as a chore: he should look forward to these times when he can please his owner and his taste buds (in that order, hopefully).

If the puppy is failing to pick up a new lesson after a few tries, back up and work on a lesson that the puppy knows well. Always end lessons on a positive note, and then go play in the yard for a while or take a walk around the neighborhood.

Everybody has an "off" day. If you come home from a particularly stressful day at work or some minor catastrophe strikes (flat tire, overdrawn checking account, extended lack of Internet connectivity), skip the training sessions and take the puppy for a walk. Rottweilers sense how their owners are feeling, and your stress or disinterest will travel down the leash. Only train the puppy when you're feeling upbeat and in the mood to make "sit" happen.

BASIC OBEDIENCE LESSONS

Patience, persistence, and consistency are the three keys to success in obedience training. Approach each command the same way every time. No matter how slowly the puppy is learning, do not lose your patience, as he will not understand the source of your frustration. When you begin on a new lesson, reward him for executing a cue properly. As you progress, you can reward every other correct behavior since your long-term goal is to have a dog who obeys cues without receiving a treat. With a Rottweiler, you will find that your puppy will learn most cues very quickly, though every dog learns at this own pace. Don't give up: a Rottweiler of average intelligence is still a very bright dog.

Now let's take a look at the basic obedience cues that every well-behaved canine must know. If you will be attending puppy kindergarten or obedience classes, you can practice these lessons at home to make sure your Rottie goes to the head of the class.

Start Here

Most training books begin with "sit," which is a perfectly good place to start, but the sit exercise isn't nearly as useful as the "take it" and "leave it" cues. These two basic cues can be used for hundreds of different occasions in your puppy's everyday life. "Take it" grants the puppy your permission to have something, and "Leave it" is essentially the positive-training way of saying "off" or "no." We will use a treat to teach the "take it." With a treat in your hand, raise your hand to the puppy's muzzle, and say "Take it." It doesn't get any easier than that, but you have to underscore the meaning of the cue. (The puppy will think that "Take it" and "Eat it" are synonymous!) After practicing "take it" a few times, hold the treat up and when the puppy anticipates and goes for the treat, close your hand and keep it closed. The puppy will likely push his snout into your hand, nuzzle it, and lick it. Just hold your hand closed and steady for a count of five or ten, and then open your hand and say "Take it." Practice this exercise a few more times, extending the length of time that you make the puppy wait for the cue and treat.

"Leave it" is essentially the opposite of "take it," but is actually just an extension of the first exercise. No dog loves the "leave it" cue, but it's the best way of teaching your puppy to drop something he shouldn't be mouthing. To begin, hold your palm out with the treat to the dog, say "Leave it." As the puppy tries to grab the treat, snap your hand close and say "Leave it" again. Now the "no fun" begins: repeat this exercise five or six times and watch your puppy react. Rottweilers know when they're being toyed with, and he'll give you a look that says, "Let's move on here." At that point, you can open your hand and say "Take it" and let him have the treat. The "Ah, ha" moment for the puppy is his recognition of the previous command: "Take it" and "Leave it" do not sound the same so they must *mean* different things. To practice this lesson, gradually extend the length of time before you allow the puppy to "take" the treat.

To go a step further with the "leave it" cue, put the puppy on a loose lead on your right side and toss a favorite toy to your left. As the puppy reacts and looks at the toy, say "Leave it" in a firm voice. If he attempts to go for it, stand in his way to prevent him from getting to it. Once he's given up, say "Take it" in a happy voice and let him go for the toy. Repeat this exercise a few times, varying the toys, so that he understands the he must wait for the "take it" cue before going for the toy.

Teaching Your Rottie to Sit

A food-motivated Rottie can learn to sit in fewer than 3 ounces of liver! A really smart Rottweiler may be able to learn to sit with just a whiff of liver, but let's not withhold the tasty stuff, lest we be covered in drool. The sit cue couldn't be simpler than just standing in front of the dog while brandishing a tiny piece of liver (or whatever your puppy loves). Lift the morsel over your pup's nose in the ideal chomping position. In a strong, clear voice say "Sit" and raise the treat. Most brilliant, hungry Rotties will master this cue instantly.

A well-behaved Rottie should be a mannerly gentleman to every young lady he meets.

In the case that your clever puppy decides to reposition himself to reach the treat, lower your hand so that he has to sit. After he's sitting for a brief second, offer him the treat as you place your hand on his collar. You want the dog to connect the cue, the treat, and your hand on his collar.

As you practice this exercise a couple times a day, you can lengthen the amount of time that your puppy sits before you offer him the treat. These extended periods (before the liver is released) may feel like an eternity to the dog, but they are the basis of the stay exercise, which we will teach next.

In addition to working on the sit cue during your designated training sessions, you should incorporate the lesson into the puppy's daily routine. Before you place the puppy's dinner bowl on the floor, tell him to sit, give it a count of five and then place his bowl on the floor and say, "OK, good dog."

The sit exercise comes naturally to many dogs, and owners should use this as a good way to conclude every lesson to end on a positive note to make your puppy feel über-smart.

A Simple Stay

Since the stay cue basically asks the Rottweiler student to "do nothing 'til you hear from me," you can imagine a bright dog wondering exactly what all the fuss is about. "Did I stop listening?" thinks the Rottweiler puppy, since he's still in a sit position and you're slowly saying "Staaaaay" to him and not giving him any other clues or cues.

The stay cue extends the previous lesson, whether it's sit, down, or stand. You're beginning with the puppy in a sit position and cuing the pup to "stay." The hand signal for stay is the same one a police officer uses to stop traffic. The puppy, who is not sure of what exactly "stay" means, will do nothing (since all you're doing is

When your puppy is focused on you in a calm, controlled setting, you should be able to teach him new commands and reinforce previous lessons.

staring at him with your hand raised). After the puppy sits and wonders for five seconds (otherwise known as staying), you break the moment in a happy voice and say "OK, good girl." Praise the puppy and give her a treat.

As you practice the sit-stay command, you can extend the length of time before you release the puppy with the "OK" command. The next step is to literally take a couple of steps backward. If the puppy gets up to follow you, step closer and say "Stay" again. For a puppy, staying for ten seconds is a great accomplishment and will give you a great foundation to build upon. If you try to make the puppy wait too long, he'll get bored and may even doze off.

The Always Important Come

As the bond with your Rottweiler develops stronger day by day, so does his need to be by your side. He has good reason to want to

Don't Bully This Cow Dog

Rottweilers don't like to be bullied! Rottweilers have a strong desire to please their masters, but they don't obey as instantly as German Shepherds or Labradors. Remember that this working breed is an independent dog who had to make decisions for himself. The Rottweiler doesn't necessarily accept that his owner knows best in every situation. Once a professional trainer/handler, such as a military service person, animal-control officer, or policeman, forges a trusting, productive partner with a Rottweiler, success is guaranteed in the most demanding work.

be close to the font of so many good things: sloppy kisses, fun games, tasty dinners, exciting outings, and, let's not forget, an unending supply of magic treats! When you call your Rottweiler to come to you, he should be curious to see what new, exciting, and tasty thing you have to offer this time.

While it's nice to have a Rottweiler who will automatically sit on cue, it's even better to have a dog who will return to you immediately when she hears "Eva, come." The come exercise is truly the most important lesson you will teach your Rottie. Coming when called can prevent a possible accident or incident, such as running into the road or chasing the neighbor's pesky cat.

A safely fenced, familiar environment (your backyard, for instance) is the best place to start practicing the come exercise. Place the puppy on her leash and let her roam around the area. With a handful of tasty treats, clap your hands and say in a happy, well-projected voice "Come, Eva!" Once she sees the treat and hears your excitement, she will gallop her way over to you to see what you're giving away this time. Offer her a treat, and then another, and another. She's hit the jackpot this time!

If she's distracted by the alluring scent or the annoying clattering of a noisy squirrel, go closer to her and give her leash a friendly tug to get her to come toward you. With her collar in one hand, give her the treat. Practice again with just as much

Walk On By

In order to keep the puppy under control on a walk, you may need some soft, smelly treats (little pieces of cheese or slices of hot dog). Make it known to the puppy that you have a pocketful of tempting goodies. Reward the puppy for staying close to you and not pulling ahead. Don't allow the puppy to bolt out ahead of you or to lag behind. You set the speed of the walk and the destination.

enthusiasm so that she comes running to you. Eventually you will only offer her a pat on the head and verbal praise instead of a treat.

Practice several times a day from the first day your puppy comes home. With lots of praise and treats, your Rottie will want to come to you every time you call him. The come exercise not only solidifies your puppy's obedience but it also strengthens your bond with your pup.

Down Exercise

It's very important that your Rottweiler is well exercised and calm before attempting to teach him the down cue. Since the down position is a compromising position for a dog, especially one as dominant as the Rottweiler, it requires patience from you and trust from your dog. It goes against the Rottweiler grain to assume a submissive position: his protective instincts necessitate that he be on his toes at all times. Naturally, puppies are more easygoing than adults in this regard, but the instincts are still there.

As the trainer, you should approach the down exercise with quiet confidence to keep your Rottweiler quiet and steady. Raise a treat over your puppy's head, and give him the sit cue. Do not give him a food reward for sitting, but instead move the treat from his nose toward his paws and then move it back between his front paws. He should move his front legs forward and his rear end to the floor. When he assumes this down position, quietly say "Down" give him the treat. You want him to remain in the down position, so do not touch him or praise him. Eventually you can add the stay cue as the puppy holds the position for five seconds or more. Give the puppy lots of happy praise after you release him from position.

Heel Exercise

We began leash training earlier, so your puppy should already be walking on a loose leash politely by your side. Formal heel training takes loose-leash walking to the next level, and while the military precision of an Obedience Trial Champion is beyond the requirements of a well-trained dog, simple heeling is not.

Don't begin the heel lesson unless your pup is well exercised; it will be very difficult to control a puppy who has not had the opportunity to burn off his excess energy. To begin, put your Rottweiler's leash on him and go into the backyard or someplace quiet with few distractions. Have your Rottweiler sit on your left side. You will need a pocketful of treats for this lesson. As you say the word "Heel," hold the treat in your left hand so that your dog can see (and smell) it. Don't let him touch it: it's enough for him to know that it's there. Take a couple steps forward while holding the treats over the dog's head (around waist high). As the dog walks forward a few steps, say "Good dog" and give him the treat.

Continue a few more steps, say "Heel" and give him the treat again as he walks. The third time, you're going to withhold the treat and try to get the dog to walk a bit farther. Teaching any dog to heel requires patience, but with persistence it is absolutely possible. Don't wait until your Rottie is a full-grown adult to begin this lesson. Begin it when your puppy is walking reliably on the leash without pulling.

Here's a fun extension of the heel exercise!

At a Glance ...

Use positive-training methods—and plenty of treats—to convey to your Rottweiler what you want. He will understand that you are in control of the things that he wants. Obedience yields good things.

Don't put off beginning your puppy's training sessions until next week. Begin it *today* (the first day he arrives). Keep lessons short so as not to bore the quick-thinking Rottie.

Puppy classes are a great choice for Rottweiler owners, but be sure to find a dog-friendly trainer who uses the right equipment and positive methods.

Every trainer must approach obedience lessons with patience, persistence, and consistency. The basic exercises include: take it, leave it, sit, stay, come, down, and heel.

CHAPTER EIGHT

Feeding and Nutrition

When it comes to feeding your Rottweiler, put your money where his mouth is! While you may decide to skimp out on your dog's brush or bed to save some money, the last place to be frugal is his food. The old adage, you get what you pay for, is almost invariably true when it comes to canine nutrition.

The best dog foods cost more because they include high-quality protein sources like beef, fish, poultry, and eggs instead of cheaper substitutes like corn, soy, and other grains. The better the

quality of protein, the better will be the food's nutrient density and digestibility. These are the three most important considerations in choosing a food: protein source, nutrients, and digestibility.

A correct diet providing the right nutrition for your Rottweiler puppy is critical to how he grows up. A diet lacking in protein or containing too much fat or carbohydrates can lead to ongoing health problems, such as diabetes, kidney disease, and orthopedic issues. High-quality foods provide the proper balance of the vitamins, minerals, and fatty acids required for a growing Rottweiler to develop healthy bone, muscle, skin, and coat.

DOG NUTRITION 101

A dog's nutritional requirements include protein, fatty acids, carbohydrates, vitamins, minerals, and, of course, water. The ten essential amino acids required by the dog are made available through high-quality protein, and it is these nutritional building blocks that provide the glucose needed for energy. Like the ten amino acids, fatty acids, which also give the dog energy, cannot be synthesized naturally in the dog's body and must be provided by the diet. Dogs who don't intake the proper amount of omega-3 fatty acids may suffer from poor eye sight and learning capability. A dog's diet should not be based on grains (aka the number-one ingredient) since they don't provide the dog with his essential amino acids. Dogs can thrive on a low-carb diet provided they are fed high-quality protein and fats. Many manufacturers include corn as the principle ingredient in their dog-food formulas because it is a source of protein though its amino-acid profile is poor. To offset this deficit, manufacturers sometimes include meat and bone meal for the additional amino acids. It's not an ideal formula for your dog, even if the label says "complete and balanced."

READING ASSIGNMENT

As you may have heard, not all dog foods are created equal, so your job as owner and consumer is to read the label to find out which products are in the formula. Manufacturers are required to list ingredients in descending order of weight or amount in the food. These foods are by definition "complete and balanced" and do not require the owner to supplement them with additional vitamins or minerals, unless your veterinarian instructs you otherwise.

Generally speaking, you should avoid foods that have a long list of ingredients that remind you of your high school chemistry class. Your dog doesn't require ethoxyquin, sodium metabisulphite, and dimethylprimidinol sulfate in his diet. Those additives aren't healthy for dogs, and neither are acronyms like BHT and BHA.

In addition to the ingredients list, the label must include the guaranteed analysis, AAFCO nutritional adequacy statement, food type, and manufacturer's contact information. If the manufacturer has complied with the AAFCO's chemical analysis of its product, the label will say: "[Brand name] is formulated to meet the nutritional levels established by the AAFCO Dog Food Nutrient Profiles for [life stage(s)]." If the company has complied with feeding-

The joys of suppertime (and soft grass) are fairly ineffable!

trial analysis of its product, the label will say, "Animal feeding tests using AAFCO procedures substantiate [brand name] provides complete and balanced nutrition for [life stage(s)]."

SELECTING THE BEST FOODS

High-quality dog-food brands produce foods for different sizes, life stages, and activity levels. Puppies, like human babies, need diets different from what adults require. Growth formulas contain protein and fat levels that are appropriate for different-sized dogs, and large dogs, like the Rottweiler, require less protein and fat during these early months of rapid growth. Since additional pounds can stress a growing puppy's joints and ligaments, keeping the puppy on the lean side is recommended by breeders and vets alike.

Selecting a brand of dog food in a large superstore is a daunting task. There are multiple aisles of food, and you could spend the better part of your week reading every label in the store. To narrow down the selection process, begin by having a conversation with your breeder or veterinarian. Do some research online and visit the different manufacturers' websites. You can also call the phone number on the package to inquire further about the contents.

A PIECE OF HISTORY

The word "Rottweiler" was first used in 1822 as a reference to a dog entered in a dog show in Heilbronn, Germany (Wurttemberg), though this dog is said to not have looked anything like the breed today. Eight years later, a caption dated 1890, describes a dog harnessed to a cart next to a peasant woman. This dog was square in build but otherwise did not resemble the breed in outward appearance.

Active dogs will eat more than less active ones. Encourage your Rottie to exercise to keep him trim and vital.

There are three basic kinds of prepared dog food: canned (wet), kibble (dry), and semi-moist. Quality canned foods are by far the most expensive option for the dog owner. They excel in digestibility and taste, though due to the high water content (70%) they are lower in protein than dry foods. Wet foods are preferred for older dogs who have become fussier, have a diminished sense of smell, or have dental problems. Far and away the most convenient and easiest to store, kibble was invented to have a longer shelf life than unprocessed food. Be sure to keep the open bag completely closed or store the kibble in an airtight container. Another advantage of dry food is the kibble's hard texture helps to keep the dog's teeth clean by scraping particles from his teeth as he chews. Semi-moist food is the "fast-food"

Human Foods to Avoid

As much as your puppy loves his dog food and treats, he will show even more interest in what you're eating. Should you succumb to those dark brown eyes, be wary that you cannot offer your puppy everything you eat. Caffeine, alcohol, and sugar, for example, are not safe for dogs to consume. That means dessert is off-limits. Never share these foods and beverages with your dog:

- avocado
- beer
- broccoli
- chocolate
- coffee
- grapes
- liquor
- macadamia nuts
- onions
- peaches and plums
- persimmons
- raisins
- soda
- sugary foods (cookies, candies, cakes)
- tea
- yeast (dough)
- wine
- xylitol (any foods containing this artificial sweetener)

of the dog world, the least nutritious and the highest in preservatives and other additives. It is the last resort for owners of ultra-fussy Rottweilers.

DAILY FEEDING ROUTINE

When the puppy first comes to your home—at around seven to nine weeks of age—you will be feeding him breakfast, lunch, and dinner. The three-meal-a-day schedule can be reduced to two meals by the time the puppy is about sixteen weeks of age, though this is a personal choice. Smaller meals served a few times a day is recommended by vets to ward off bloat. Free-feeding (leaving a bowl of dry food on the floor all day) is discouraged for the Rottweiler, as this can lead to picky eating and food possessiveness. It is better to place the bowl on the floor for the puppy, allow him ten minutes to eat, and then remove the bowl. For most Rotties, ten minutes in front of a food bowl usually means two minutes of eating his food and eight minutes of cleaning the bowl. Rotties tend to be fast eaters, but give the puppy time so that he doesn't feel compelled to eat quickly. If the puppy inhales his food inside a couple of minutes, you should add another scoop to his bowl. Of course, if the puppy is still eating after ten minutes, allow him to finish his portion. If he walks away without finishing his food, you can offer him a bit less next time. It's important to pay attention to how much the puppy is eating. If you have a second dog in the house, be sure that the puppy is getting all his food (and only his food).

If you've chosen a high-quality dog food, the package will make recommendations for how much food to offer. Remember that a cup is a unit of measurement and not any mug you grab out of your cabinet.

If you're considering free-feeding for purposes of convenience, don't start until the puppy is completely house-trained. Scheduled meals help to predict elimination times, which is a real advantage during house training.

WAIST WATCHERS

If you wish to add a little cooked or raw fresh meat to your dog's kibble, you certainly won't hear any complaints from your Rottweiler. Many breeders recommend adding not just meat but also vegetables and cottage cheese to puppy diets. A growing puppy requires twice as many calories (per pound of body weight) as an adult dog. An active young adult Rottweiler, weighing 70 pounds, requires a daily caloric intake of about 2,000 calories.

It's a rare Rottie who doesn't approach mealtimes with gusto, but fussy eaters do exist. Many owners add a scoop of a high-quality canned food to their dogs' kibble to add a little excitement to dinnertime. Don't overdo the toppings: you may develop a fussy dog who won't eat his kibble without the extras. Offer a topping every other day or just twice

"What do you mean 'no seconds'?" Don't overfeed your Rottweiler, no matter how disarming his "hungry" gaze.

a week. If you offer it at every meal, your very cute, very smart, very manipulative Rottweiler will work all his black and tan magic to get his favorite chicken and cheese toppings daily.

On this same note, another important "don't" regards overfeeding. Because the Rottweiler is broad and "big boned," as parents and owners are apt to say, it's harder to tell whether a puppy is a good healthy weight or a little chubby. Overfeeding a puppy doesn't make him bigger, stronger, and healthier—it makes him fat. Too much weight on a puppy stresses his growing frame and can hinder his proper development.

If you can't see your Rottweiler's waist, he is too fat: he should not resemble a bratwurst! Most owners can't see the extra pounds on their babies. Veterinary schools and associations are encouraging vets to become more involved in nutritional assessment and counseling, and a good veterinarian will ask you what you are feeding your dog. He or she knows that the quality of a dog's food affects his response to disease and injury and is critical to maintaining good overall health. Don't be shy about asking for your vet's opinion about feeding your dog and his growth and condition, and tell him you're prepared for a candid response. The vet should be able to determine your dog's body condition score (BCS) and muscle condition score (MCS) to evaluate his body fat and muscle condition. Palpating the dog's ribs will tell the vet whether there is excess fat covering them and whether his waist and abdominal tuck-up are discernible.

RISK FACTORS FOR BLOAT

The American Kennel Club has launched a research initiative through the AKC Canine Health Foundation on this health issue. While risk factors have been identified, scientists still do not understand the exact cause of bloat or GDV (gastric dilatation and volvulus). Large, deep-chested dogs, including the Rottweiler, are more predisposed to the condition due to their anatomical structure, but other factors cited include feeding practices, exercise, stress, and genetic background. According to the American Veterinary Medical Association (AVMA), bloat occurs when gas and/or food stretches the dog's stomach to many times its normal size. The result is unbearable abdominal pain, as the stomach tends to rotate up on itself, cutting off blood supply and the exit route for gas, often leading to death if emergency surgery is not immediately available. The AVMA recommends that Rottweiler owners offer the dog's food in multiple smaller meals and discourage eating too swiftly.

Veterinarians recommend that owners remove their dogs' water bowl during mealtimes, because they believe that limiting water at mealtimes can prevent bloat. Additionally, owners should not add water to dry food, especially if citric acid is used in the kibble as a preservative.

SOME FAQS ABOUT FOOD

Should I feed my Rottweiler the exact amount listed on the package or can of food?

The amount listed is a "suggestion" and is meant for a dog who is active and healthy. Many veterinarians believe that "less is more," or better yet: "lean is more"!

How much protein does my dog need?

A puppy requires more protein than an adult dog. Puppies need 22 to 32% protein, compared to adults needing 15 to 30%. The amount of protein in a dog food is not as important as the quality of the source.

Can I feed my Rottweiler a vegetarian diet?

While humans can choose to exist on a vegetarian diet, no dog would ever choose a life without meat. The dog's digestive system is fairly inefficient at assimilating plant matter as a source of high-quality protein, which means that a vegetarian diet for a dog would have to contain enough digestible protein to provide the essential amino acids. (Nutritionists say that vitamin D supplementation would be required as well.) The dog's ability to digest the protein source plays an important role in the dog's health, as quality protein is required for the dog to grow and develop properly as well as to heal and maintain healthy coat, nails, and connective tissue. For an adult dog to thrive on a plant-based diet, he must receive 10% of his calories from protein. A senior dog, however, requires half of his calories to come from a quality protein source. The dog's stomach is not designed to breakdown cellulose the way an omnivore's digestive tract can, and the canine pancreas is not equipped to secrete cellulose to process glucose for energy.

Is chicken meal an acceptable ingredient in my dog's food?

Meal is essentially a dry, ground version of a product, such as chicken, lamb, or corn, with the water and fat removed. Chicken meal, then, is chicken that's been rendered, a process the separates fat and removes water to form a concentrated version of the protein. Meal is not the same as "by-product," which has less stringent guidelines and usually contains organ meats and possibly some extraneous materials (such as hooves, horns, hair, and stomach contents). Meat by-products are less digestible than meal but still provide an ample source of protein.

Should I look for a dog food that's labeled "complete and balanced"?

Yes, the Association of American Feed Control Officials (AAFCO) establishes nutritional standards for complete and balanced pet foods. By law, a manufacturer may only use the term "complete and balanced" if its product has met the nutritional requirements established by the AAFCO through feeding trials. Some companies do not use the feeding-trials method where actual dogs are fed the food; instead they use a laboratory test to calculate the nutritional value of the food. These foods then "meet the nutritional levels established by the AAFCO" but cannot use the term "complete and balanced." That said, the term does not guarantee that it will provide your dog with optimal nutrition, especially if the first ingredient on the label is not meat or meat meal.

Discourage your dog from vigorous play and exercise before and after mealtimes. While veterinarians continue to debate the definitive causes of bloat in dogs, Rottie owners are wise to observe all possible precautions.

Are eggs good for my dog?

Eggs are a superb choice of protein for your dog. Egg whites in particular provide all of the amino acids your dog requires and is considered the yardstick by which other protein sources are measured. When preparing an egg for your adult dog, chop up the shell and fold it into your Rottie's omelet: he'll enjoy the crunch and the calcium boost. Puppies do not need additional calcium in their diets.

Should I look for dog foods called "premium" or "ultra premium"?

These terms are used by many manufacturers and do not guarantee any particular quality, though the price might be higher nonetheless. The FDA and the AAFCO do not define these terms and therefore they are not regulated. Likewise, terms like "organic," "holistic," and "human-grade" are unregulated in dog food and don't guarantee the actual quality of the food.

Does the word "natural" on a pet food label have any meaning?

Unlike "organic" and "human-grade," the term "natural" is defined by the AAFCO as "derived solely from plant, animal or mined sources, either in its unprocessed state or having been subject to physical processing, heat processing, rendering, purification, extraction, hydrolysis, enzymolysis or fermentation, but not having been produced by or subject to a chemically synthetic process and not containing any additives or processing aids that are chemically synthetic except in amounts as might occur unavoidably in good manufacturing practices." A "natural" food, however, can include the addition of vitamins and minerals to meet the definition of "complete and balanced," though the label must include a disclaimer.

Will my Rottweiler get bored if I feed him the same food every day?

Although dogs don't require the same variation in their diets that humans do, dogs can get tired of the "same old chow." A good plan is to stick with a brand that the dog likes and that is providing him with optimal health and condition and switch the flavors of the cans and/or kibble. Adding some quality protein (like fresh cooked chicken or low-fat hamburger) to his bowl on occasion will also add some interest to your Rottie's mealtimes.

Should I supplement by dog's diet with vitamins and minerals?

Like most Americans you probably take a daily multivitamin, and you're wondering if your Rottie can use a little boost of vitamin C and vitamin E. The best answer is no, unless your vet recommends supplements for a particular need. Your Rottweiler will get his daily supply of vitamins and minerals from his food and doesn't need additional supplements. In fact, excess calcium can cause complications in a growing Rottweiler, and too much vitamin A and vitamin D can interfere with bones, joints, and muscle development. Talk to your vet before offering your dog any kind of supplement.

Should I attempt to cook for my dog?

Many Rottweiler owners have cooked for their dogs for years and have enjoyed

great success! If done correctly, a homecooked diet can provide ideal nutrition for the Rottweiler. Replacing commercial diets with homemade diets is a major commitment and a choice that will require significant effort and research to do correctly. No doubt your Rottweiler will approve and won't be shy about telling you that your cooked chicken tastes a lot better than the dehydrated kibble in his bowl, the one with the sprayed-on nutrients. There are many recipes for dog foods online or in books, though proceed with caution as often these sources don't give specific instructions for feeding dogs of different sizes. If you are committed to the concept of cooking for your dog, you are best to consult with your vet, an experienced Rottweiler breeder, or a board-certified veterinary nutritionist who can outline a diet suitable for your Rottweiler at his current age. Visit www.acvn.org for a directory of professionals to assist you.

At a Glance ...

Providing your Rottweiler with the best possible nutrition begins with selecting a top-quality food. The higher the quality of ingredients in the food, the more costly it will likely be.

. . . .

Do you remember what an amino acid is? A quick brush-up course on canine nutrition will go a long way to help you understand what your Rottie needs to thrive. It's all about excellent protein, carbs, fats, and vitamins and minerals.

. . . .

Establish a daily feeding routine for your Rottie, two or three meals per day, depending on the puppy's age. Free-feeding is not recommended for pups.

. . . .

Avoid overfeeding your dog, as obesity can shorten a dog's life. Also, be aware of the dangers of bloat for deep-chested dogs like Rottweilers.

CHAPTER NINE

Coat Care and More

Rottweiler owners don't need to fuss too much to keep their dogs looking their best. This black and tan wonder is a true natural beauty, a dog who needs no more than a onceover brushing and an occasional bath to turn heads on the street or in the show ring. Show dogs necessarily are bathed more than pet dogs, since handlers do better when they exhibit clean dogs to a judge. Fortunately, your Rottie will likely only need a bath a few times a year, though some Rotties would prefer a bath daily!

Here a Hair, There a Hair

Shedding is an ongoing process for most dogs, and the Rottweiler will drop his tiny black hairs 365 days a year. Any dog with a double coat—a thick downy undercoat beneath a harsh top coat—blows his full coat seasonally (spring and fall). Keep your Rottweiler's slicker brush or Furminator on hand: it's faster and more efficient than vacuuming every room of the house!

BRUSHING

Set aside time twice a week to brush the Rottweiler's coat. If you brush him nice and slow, give him encouragement and a treat or two, grooming sessions will become one of your dog's favorite times. During most of the year, grooming isn't much of a commitment on the owner's part since it takes about three minutes.

The Rottweiler possesses a double coat, which means that underneath the black and tan outer coat (that you can see) is a soft undercoat (that you can't see, unless it's shedding time). In color, the undercoat is tan, black, or gray and is present mainly on the neck and thighs. If you live in a colder climate, your Rottie will develop more undercoat than if he lived in a more temperate climate. During shedding times, the undercoat loosens, and you'll see small gray clouds floating in every room. To minimize coat blowing around the house and to assist the dog with his new coat, you will need to brush the coat daily, or even twice a day once the shedding is in full swing. Fortunately for Rottie owners, there's not nearly as much

The Rottie is an easycare companion when it comes to grooming. Brushing the coat (and the teeth) take little time at all.

coat as with long-haired breeds like Golden Retrievers or Samoyeds. Begin brushing the puppy with the combination brush—the one with soft to medium bristles on one side and a pin brush on the other. Introduce the puppy to grooming early on so that he accepts the routine. Let the puppy sniff the brush, but don't surrender it to him as a chew toy. He needs to understand that grooming is not a game and that he must sit (or stand) calmly while he is brushed. Rottie puppies love attention, and a soft brush on the puppy's coat is a pleasant sensation the puppy will learn to enjoy.

Although the Rottweiler coat is relatively low-maintenance, many owners like to give the coat a daily onceover with a grooming mitt. This two-minute process is a lot easier than running the vacuum, so it's time well spent. A grooming mitt, equipped with rubbed tips, fits over any hand (usually right hand) and can be fastened with straps. While removing the dead hair, the mitt gives the dog a nice massage. The dead hair is easily collected from the mitt, so clean it after each use.

After a day playing at the beach, your Rottie may need a good brushing and possibly a warm bath to remove the sand and salt.

A GOOD DAY FOR A BATH

Even though your Rottweiler doesn't require frequently bathing, bath day does take some preparation. Choose a nice sunny day (with no rain in the forecast) to bathe your Rottweiler. It is much easier to bathe and dry a Rottweiler outdoors than to attempt it in your own bathroom or kitchen.

Autumn is a good time for photographing your Rottweilers in piles of leaves—and for checking their coats for parasites and debris.

For quick cleanups, you can use the mitt to collect dropped coat from your furniture or carpets, if you like.

To groom the adult coat, an undercoat rake does a great job at removing the loose undercoat and avoiding mats from developing. The rake has stainless steel edges or rotating pins, depending on the model. A slicker brush, which includes steel pins embedded into a foam or rubber base, will also remove the undercoat. A traditional bristle brush, preferably with firm, short bristles, spaced closely together, can also be used on the adult coat. Both brushes are effective and will not disturb the outer coat while collecting the downy undercoat.

When brushing the dog's coat, go slowly and brush with the grain of the coat. Go easy and talk sweetly to your dog. You want him to know that this is about him and that he's special. Don't brush too hard or for too long.

BATHING

The Rottweiler, equipped with one of nature's self-cleaning coats, doesn't require frequent bathing. Dust and dirt falls off the breed's harsh jacket once it dries. Unless the puppy paddles across a mud puddle or swims across a swamp, he will only need to be bathed a few times a year. After the dog's fall and spring sheddings, at the end of the bitch's completed heat cycle, and after an encounter with a skunk or a stinky substance in the grass are all good times to bathe the dog.

Purchase a dog shampoo and conditioner designed specifically for dogs. Human shampoo and soap products are not designed to wash fur and may be too harsh for a dog's coat.

Before you begin bathing the dog, make sure you have everything you need, including a few bath towels to dry the dog, a hose (or hose attachment), bucket, washcloth, etc. You don't want to have to abandon a soaking wet Rottie while you go hunting for a towel. Keep the dog on a leash so that you have some control of him. Ideally, a friend or family member can assist you. The more prepared you are, the smoother the bath will go. On warm days, you will be able to bathe the Rottweiler outdoors, using the hose and a large basin.

Be sure to brush the dog's coat out thoroughly before bathing begins. Wet the coat completely with lukewarm water (warm to your touch, not hot). Begin applying the shampoo on the dog's body, saving the head and face for last. Massage the shampoo into a firm lather and then rinse the soap out thoroughly with a shower attachment or hose. Wash the face carefully with a soapy washcloth. Soap residue left in the coat can cause skin irritation.

Some Rottweilers don't mind taking a bath: some adore it and others despise getting wet. This is more an individual dog preference than a breed trait. Although Rottweilers weren't bred to retrieve ducks from a lake or rescue shipwrecked sailors, some take to water like Labradors and Newfs! It's always a good idea to start exposing the puppy to the bath early on, and offer him treats for standing still in the tub or basin. Simultaneously lather the puppy with soap and sweet talk for the best results.

Once the dog has been bathed and rinsed thoroughly, it's time to dry him. The dog's first instinct once he's out of the tub is to shake his coat out. That's fine in the backyard, but not indoors, so you'll have to be ready with a heavy towel to delay the shaking.

NAILS

While bathing isn't a universally despised canine activity, nail clipping usually is. Most dogs do not like to surrender their paws to a nail clipper: it doesn't make good doggy sense. Owners should begin working with their Rottweiler's feet as soon as they come home. Massaging the feet and touching the nails are good ways to

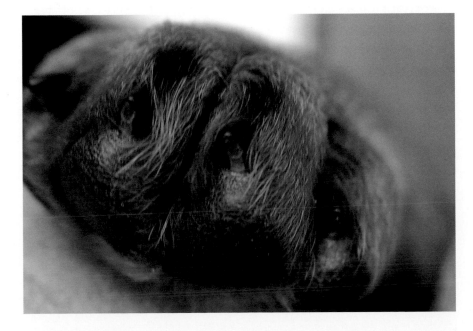

Keep your Rottie's toenails short and neat. Untrimmed nails can lead to splayed feet and discomfort for your dog.

Be Smart about Grooming

The smarter you are about Rottie grooming, the easier it will be on you and the dog. Here's ten tips to get you started:

1. Use shampoo formulated for dogs; human products will dry out your dog's coat. Pet shops sell shampoos and conditioners made for dogs.

2. Your Rottie's teeth should be brushed every day; use toothpaste made for dogs as yours will make your dog choke and isn't designed for canines' canines.

3. Begin handling the puppy's feet and mouth from the day he comes home to desensitize him to squirming when you need to check his paw or teeth, trim his nails, or brush his teeth.

4. You will have to clip your dog's nails less frequently if he walks on pavement, though the dewclaws will still require trimming.

5. Not all grooming salons welcome Rottweilers; save the money and the aggravation and do it at home.

6. Rottweilers shed every day, not just twice a year; during the shedding periods, the whole undercoat is blown.

7. If you put cotton in your Rottie's ears before bath time, don't forget to take it out or he will stop listening to you.

8. Always brush the Rottweiler's coat thoroughly before giving him a bath.

9. If your dog is scooting his bottom across the carpet, he's trying to relieve his anal sacs. Bring him to the vet to express the glands.

10. Buy a flea comb to check your Rottweiler's coat for fleas and ticks. The naked eye can't detect much a deep black coat.

desensitize the puppy to foot handling and to build his trust in you. Offer him a treat for allowing you to hold his paw. For an adult dog who hates his feet being touched, not even a homemade cookie is enough to bribe him to hand over his paw. The owner's goal is to make the puppy (or dog) believe that nail trimming is associated with positive things (praise, treats, attention, a new Kong).

Rottweiler owners have the further disadvantage of dealing with nails that are solid black, making it impossible to see where the dog's quick begins. The quick is a blood vessel that runs through each nail. The best way to clip the Rottie's nails is to proceed slowly, taking off a sliver off at a time. If you cut into the quick, the nail will bleed and your dog will likely yelp and yank his foot from you. Have a styptic powder or pencil available in case you cut the quick and need to clot the bleeding. (Offer you pup an apology cookie, too.)

The thought of making the dog's nail bleed can make an owner queasy about nail clipping, which only serves to make matters worse. Your Rottweiler will sense that you're uneasy about the task and respond accordingly. Trimming your own finger nails is not painful and it's no different for the dog. As long as you proceed slowly and gently, you should have no problems.

Purchase a guillotine-type nail clipper, the type that has a hole for the tip of the dog's nail to be inserted, as opposed to the scissors style. The guillotine clipper is the safer way to cut the dog's nails, as the scissors can crush the nail and cause the dog discomfort. Dogs who are exercised on pavement will require less frequent nail clipping, though the dog's dewclaws, if present, will need to be clipped. The first time you clip his nails, quit after two or three. You can continue tomorrow. Don't try to do all twenty (or twenty-two) in one sitting!

If you are still uncomfortable trimming the dog's nails, request that your veterinarian trim the nails when you visit. You can also seek out the services of a professional grooming parlor for your Rottie's pedicures.

SMILE, ROTTIE!

Brushing the Rottweiler's teeth is essential to his ongoing health, but how often do you need to brush his teeth? Humans usually brush their teeth twice a day, in the morning and at night. Most owners aren't able to find the time to brush their dogs' teeth daily, but every other day is perfectly acceptable. The ASPCA recommends owners brush their dogs' teeth "several times a week." Failure to brush a dog's teeth can lead to bacteria collecting at the gum line and plaque and tartar building up on the teeth. Periodontal disease, which can lead to further health problems, is the unfortunate result of poor dental hygiene in dogs. Veterinarians estimate that 85 percent of dogs over five years of age exhibit some degree of periodontal disease. Brushing can prevent the onset of this disease in your Rottweiler.

Agouti Coloration

Genetically speaking, the Rottweiler's coloration belongs to the agouti series, as the traditional tan points are almost the bottom recessive in the series, meaning that a dog must have two copies of the tan-point gene in order for the tan points to appear. All Rottweilers, Doberman Pinschers, and Manchester Terriers carry *only* the tan-point allele.

Brushing your Rottweiler's teeth a few times a week will keep you both smiling for years to come.

Pet-supply stores sell a variety of doggy toothbrushing devices, including specially designed angulated brushes and ridged caps that fit over a finger, as well as dog toothpaste (flavored in liver or chicken instead of spearmint). Some owners like to use a piece of gauze to clean the teeth or even a sponge. Choose whichever device you're most comfortable with or that your Rottie tolerates the best.

Get your puppy accustomed to having his mouth handled when he's young. Offer the puppy a treat after he's allowed you to touch his muzzle or rub a finger on his gums or teeth. Increase the length of time you touch the puppy's muzzle and mouth before offering him a treat. You will not be able to brush your dog's teeth if he's unwilling to allow you. Make the Rottweiler know that good things will result from his cooperation to let you touch his mouth and brush his teeth. Don't try to brush every tooth in your puppy's mouth at your first attempt. Spend a minute or two with the brush, and then go for a walk.

Whatever you do, don't struggle with your Rottweiler to force him to accept tooth brushing (or nail clipping). Your success has to stem from the dog's cooperation

Drop-eared breeds are generally more prone to ear infections than are dogs with erect ears. Get in the habit of checking your dog's ears regularly to be proactive against possible problems.

Healthy Ears

In perfect harmony, yeast and bacteria live in a healthy dog's ears. An ear infection occurs when the yeast or bacteria offsets the balance. Yeast overgrowing causes the typical odor associated with ear infections, and the yeast infection usually turns into a bacterial infection. When treating an ear infection, be sure to follow up until the infection is completely cleared up. It's the owner's failure to continue the treatment that is responsible for the infection's recurring.

and enjoyment (otherwise known as tolerance) of the grooming procedure. Trying to wrestle the dog to the ground while brandishing a toothbrush may lead to aggressive behavior from the dog.

EARS

Good ear hygiene won't improve how well your Rottweiler hears your training cues, but it will ward off possible infections. Ear infections may be more common in drop-eared or floppy-eared dogs like the Rottweiler because the ear canals don't get as much ventilation as those of upright-eared dogs. You can purchase a mild solution for cleaning your dog's ears to remove any dirt, yeast, or wax buildup. Don't purchase a medicated solution unless your veterinarian recommends one. Likewise, you can make your own ear-cleaning solution by combining white or apple cider vinegar and purified water (in equal parts) or hydrogen peroxide and purified water (in equal parts). You can also use Witch Hazel or a diluted tea tree oil solution to clean your dog's ears and prevent possible infections.

At a Glance ...

The Rottweiler sheds his coat twice a year, usually in spring and fall, though all double-coated dogs shed a little all year long.

. . . .

To minimize shedding and give the dog's coat a healthy, glistening appearance, brush the coat a couple of times a week. In addition to the coat, owners must care for their dogs' teeth, nails, ears, and eyes.

. . . .

Purchase the best-quality grooming tools possible. For the puppy, a combination pin brush and bristle brush; for the adult, a slicker brush or an undercoat rake, a grooming mitt, as well as specially made nail clippers, a toothbrush and toothpaste.

. . . .

Bathe your Rottie as needed with a shampoo made especially for dogs and a bucketful of patience and treats.

CHAPTER TEN

A Long, Healthy Life

If you've begun your life as a Rottweiler owner with a healthy and sound puppy from a breeder, you are ahead of the game. We are the daily caregivers of the dogs who have entrusted their lives to us, and it's up to us to provide the best possible care that we are able. That includes being a responsible, well-informed dog parent who will keep your Rottie trim and active, visiting a vet at least once a year, and being attentive to the dog's dietary, emotional, and bodily needs.

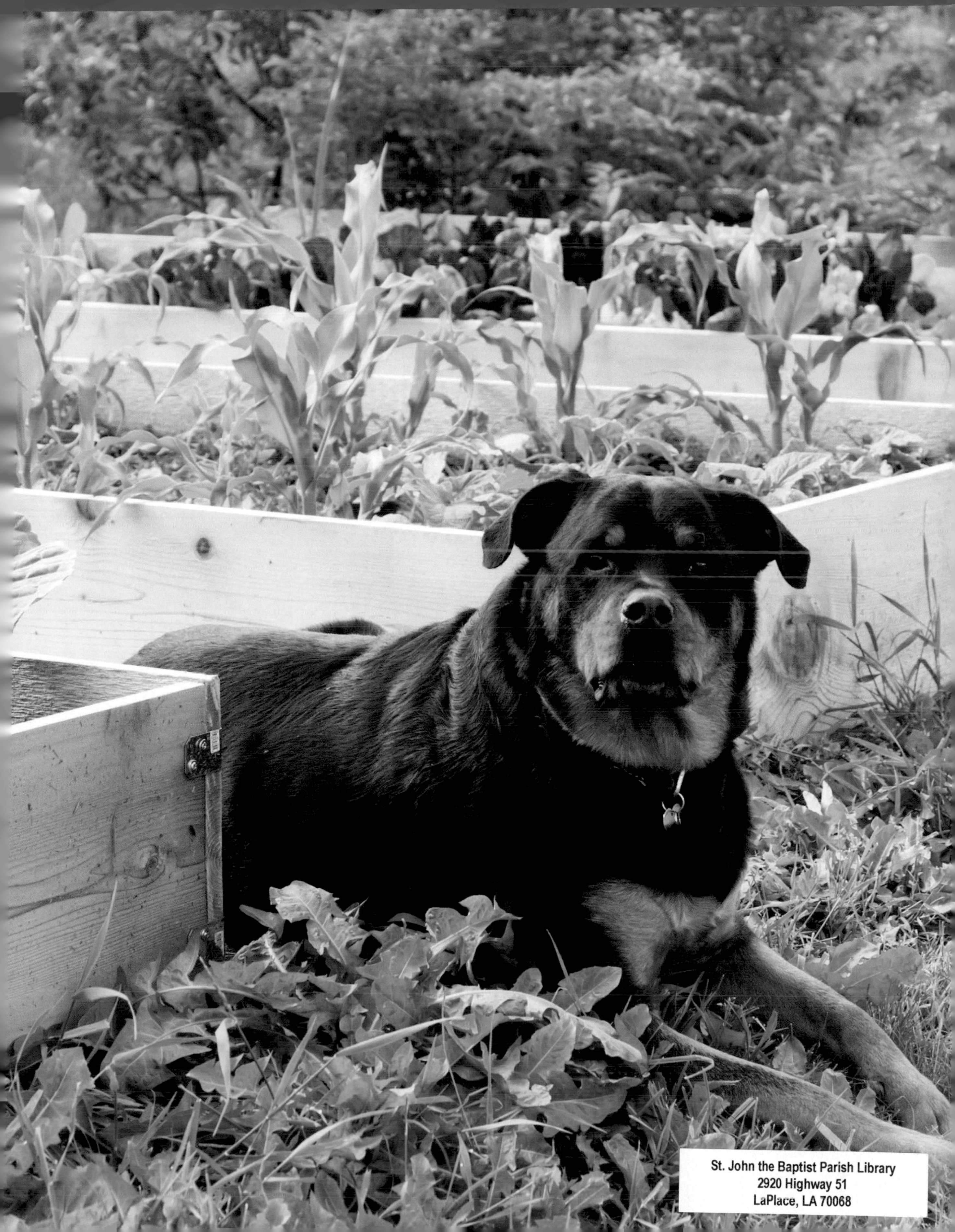

Rotties live to move! Once you find the activity that your dog loves, make it a part of your weekly routine.

Keep a close eye on your Rottweiler when he's feeling well so you recognize when things are "off." A healthy puppy will:

- have a moist nose, with no signs of dryness or any mucous buildup
- be fit and able to amble freely about without favoring one side over the other, limping, or hobbling
- have clean, pink ears, without any bad odor, discharge, or waxy buildup

Health Insurance

The time to insure your Rottweiler's ongoing health is now. Pet health insurance is a relatively new concept, but more and more dog owners have been taking advantage of the excellent options available on the market. Invest while your Rottweiler is still a puppy and avoid any unwelcome surprises down the road. Do some research and ask your veterinarian which providers he or she recommends. Plans vary in terms of what they cover, but at the very least you want a policy that covers emergency and major health crisis. Pet Partners, the AKC's pet healthcare provider, has been working with AKC dog owners since 2003, and you can learn more about them at www.akcpethealthcare.com.

- possess a clean, shiny coat, without any parasite droppings
- have healthy-looking gums and teeth and no bad breath
- look at you with bright, clear eyes, without cloudiness or any sign of discharge
- eat and drink normally without excessive thirst or fussiness
- have normal bowel movements

KEEP IT MOVING!

As Newton's law of motion teaches us, "An object in motion stays in motion," so get yourself and your Rottie off the couch and go for a walk. Just as you grab your sneakers and head to the gym, your Rottweiler needs to get outside and move. Many people have taken their cue from their MDs: exercise can save your life! According to a 2013 research report from Ramblers and Macmillan Cancer Support, a British charitable association, a twenty-minute daily walk could save 37,000 people annually from succumbing to cancer, heart disease, and stroke.

Exercise is vital for human and canine alike, so get motivated and grab your sneakers and your Rottie's leash. Given the rowdy, ready-to-go nature of the Rottweiler, your dog won't need much prodding to get outside to play for hours on end. In addition to long walks and jogs, your adult Rottweiler will enjoy swimming; fetching Frisbees, balls, and sticks; hiking and biking; and any other activity you can dream up. Remember not to overdo it with young dogs or dogs who are a bit out of shape. Take it easy and work out a realistic, daily routine. Just as the right diet is critical to your dog's help, so too is the right mix of physical exercise and mental stimulation. By keeping your dog in motion, you will keep your dog young at heart and body for years to come. And you too.

SELECTING A VETERINARIAN

It is your responsibility to find a good veterinarian whom you can rely upon for the best possible care throughout your dog's life. A qualified vet will play a huge role in the life of your Rottweiler, and you will come to depend on him or her for advice and guidance for years to come.

Don't wait for your puppy to come home to find a vet. Begin your search as soon as you've decided upon a puppy. The most obvious consideration for choosing a vet is the location of the practice. Twenty minutes is a reasonable distance to drive to reach your vet since any farther would be a disadvantage in an emergency situation. Owners who live in the suburbs have more options than those who live in rural areas where there are fewer practices close by.

Ask your friends and family for references for vets in your area. Ask about office hours, flexibility of policies and appointments, and how knowledgeable and personable are the vets and staff members. Before visiting the office, you can do your own research by contacting your state's veterinary medical board and the American Animal Hospital Association to confirm the vet's certification. The AKC website also has a list of qualified veterinarians in the AKC Veterinary Network.

Make an appointment to visit the facility, and let the staff know that you would like to speak to the vet for a few minutes. On your first visit to the vet's office, you'll get a good feel for the staff and the facility. Is it cold and unfriendly or welcoming

Miami Heat

Black dogs attract the sunlight and can heat up fast in the summer sun. Be sure to provide lots of cool water and shade for your Rottie on hot, humid days. Many Rottweilers enjoy sunbathing—the breed was the number-two registered dog in Miami, Florida, in 2012--but owners have to be aware of signs of heatstroke and know what to do if their dog is having a sun emergency.

Your puppy's first ride to the veterinarian's office will be less stressful if you transport him in his crate.

and cheerful? Are there many clients in the waiting room? Are the receptionists and vet techs helpful and interested in you? Ask about payment policies, fees, credit cards, and billing.

When bringing your puppy to meet the vet for the first time, you can observe how he or she interacts with your Rottie. By transporting your puppy to the vet in his crate you can avoid unwanted encounters with unknown dogs. Your puppy, too, will be more content in the familiar surroundings of his crate. Some puppies react negatively to the sounds and smells of a veterinary office. Anything you can do to keep your puppy feeling safe and comfortable will help to make the experience more positive.

Many veterinary clinics offer other services, such as 24-hour emergency care, grooming, and boarding. If the clinic is a large facility that includes multiple vets, other specialists and special testing equipment may be available onsite.

VACCINATIONS

Most puppies receive their first set of shots at around six weeks of age. Your breeder should provide you with a list of which shots the puppy has received and tell you when the next rounds are due. Your vet will thoroughly examine the puppy at his first visit, checking over his general condition and all his vitals. Ear mites are a common puppy health concern, as are roundworms. The vet should check the puppy's ears and examine a stool sample (which you brought along). Although breeders have puppies wormed prior to releasing to homes, the vet still must check for possible internal parasites.

The puppy's initial vaccination schedule is complete by the time the puppy is sixteen weeks of age. Annual boosters are required for some vaccinations, but discuss the ongoing schedule with your vet. Depending on where you live and how frequently your dog will encounter other dogs (at dog parks, shows, or day care), your vet may recommend a kennel cough booster.

The American Veterinary Medical Association (AVMA) recommends four core vaccines, all of which are highly recommended to protect canines against dangerous, potentially deadly, diseases. Canine distemper, canine parvovirus, canine adenovirus (type 2), and rabies are all highly contagious diseases that affect both puppies and adult dogs. While none of the core vaccinations should be considered optional, rabies immunization is required by law in all fifty states. Most municipalities will not issue a dog license without proof of a current rabies inoculation.

Noncore vaccines, recommended by the AVMA only in particular circumstances where risk is believed to be present, include measles, Bordetella bronchiseptica (commonly known as kennel cough), canine parainfluenza virus, canine influenza virus, leptospirosis interrogans, canine coronavirus, and Lyme disease (borreliosis). Your veterinarian will advise you about which of these you should consider immunizing against.

The AVMA recommends that veterinarians vaccinate adult dogs every three years instead of annually, although the rabies vaccination is regulated by state and your

Rottweiler Health Foundation

The Rottweiler Health Foundation (RHF) is an independent not-for-profit organization that seeks to promote and financially support Rottweiler health research. It is funded through ARC member donations and individual contributions. Among the RHF's goals is to educate the public about care and health-related issues, to establish a national database of resource materials, and to further the understanding of diseases and defects that affect the Rottweiler breed. To become a member or make a contribution, visit www.rottweilerhealth.org.

vet will know the requirement. Your vet will advise you about the best vaccination schedule for your Rottweiler, assisting to keep you up to date on required boosters. However, it is completely your responsibility to get your dog to the vet in a timely fashion. Beyond a postcard, email, or telephone call reminding you about what shots are due, the vet has no further obligation. For the continued safety and health of your dog, keep his shots current.

NOBODY LIKES A PARASITE!

Avoiding the cost and inconvenience of "de-fleaing" your house and dog should be enough inspiration for any sensible dog owner to take full advantage of modern scientific advances. Who'd ever think you'd be singing the praises of cutting-edge parasitologists! Almost nothing compares to the nuisance of having to set off four flea bombs in your house while you drive your ungleeful, flea-ful Rottweiler to the grooming salon to be dipped!

The "great outdoors" is much greater without fleas and ticks. Take precautions to protect your Rotties from irritating crawlies.

Core Vaccines

Check with your vet, but all puppies should receive vaccines for the following diseases:

CONDITION	TREATMENT	PROGNOSIS	VACCINE NEEDED
ADENOVIRUS-2	No curative therapy for infectious hepatitis; treatment geared toward minimizing neurologic effects, shock, hemorrhage, secondary infections	Highly contagious and can be mild to rapidly fatal	Recommended (immunizes against adenovirus-1, the agent of infectious canine hepatitis)
DISTEMPER	No specific treatment; supportive treatment (IV fluids, antibiotics)	High mortality rates	Highly recommended
PARVOVIRUS-2	No specific treatment; supportive treatment (IV fluids, antibiotics)	Highly contagious to young puppies; high mortality rates	Highly recommended
RABIES	No treatment	Fatal	Required

Veterinarians have always preached the gospel of preventive health care, and there are a number of simple ways to avoid "flea D-Day" in your home. Topical solutions applied to your dog's coat (usually behind his neck, where he can't lick) or oral medications have become the dog owner's arsenal to combat fleas. Discuss the options with your veterinarian and begin a parasite-prevention routine as soon as recommended. Some applications can be applied to puppies as young as six weeks of age, others not until the puppy is six months old.

Watching your dog scratching at his sides or biting at his legs and belly are sure signs that your dog is dealing with some tiny vampire arthropods! You may find small remnants of fleas on your Rottie's coat, usually droppings or possibly the insects themselves. Given the Rottweiler's jet black coat, fleas aren't easy to spot. If you see a flea hop off your dog—they're wingless, so thankfully they don't fly—you'll find that it's difficult to kill it. Their bodies withstand pressure, making it hard to squeeze them. The easiest way to kill fleas is to drop them in a cup of bleach or soapy water or possibly to collect them with tape.

Like fleas, ticks carry disease and bite your dog to ingest his blood. A flea or tick infestation can ravage your dog's coat, and if your Rottweiler is allergic to flea bites, it can be a real catastrophe. A dog suffering from a flea-bite allergy will engage in extreme itching, usually on the rear part of the body. Scabs and hair loss are common, as are infection and lesions in extreme cases. In addition to topical solutions and medicated shampoos, your dog may require antihistamines or even steroids to overcome the infestation and infection.

While fleas can cause your dog great discomfort and even lead to flea-bite anemia and a tapeworm infestation, they can transmit bacteria to humans and cause endemic or murine typhus. And let's not even talk about the plague (caused by the bacterium *Yersinia pesitis* from a flea bite). Tick-borne diseases are not uncommon in the United States. According to the Center for Disease Control, no fewer than eleven diseases are caused by pathogens carried by ticks. Lyme disease and anaplasmosis are caused by the tick *Ixodes scapularis* in the northeastern U.S. and upper Midwestern U.S. and by the tick *Ixodes pacificus* in the Pacific U.S. In the southcentral and eastern U.S., ehrlichiosis is caused by *Ambylomma americanum*, the lone star tick. Rocky Mountain spotted fever can be caused by a number of ticks in North, Central, and South America.

The American Kennel Club's Canine Health Foundation recognizes the seriousness of tick-borne disease in dogs: "The broad spectrum of possible symptoms associated with tick-borne diseases in dogs (including no symptoms) makes annual screening for tick disease a vital component of your pet's annual veterinary exam." Always check your dog for ticks whenever he's out in a grassy field or the near the woods: tick season goes from spring to fall, or all year in more temperate climates. Usually black or dark brown, ticks range in size from a pinhead to a grape when they are embedded in the dog's skin. A tick can spread disease to your dog once it has been embedded for 24 hours.

From bugs to worms: internal parasites can be even worse, and the roundworm is the most commonly encountered in dogs. A stool sample will provide your vet with all the evidence he or she needs to determine if your Rottweiler has a worm infestation. Tapeworms, like roundworms, are large enough to be seen by the naked eye in a stool sample. Hookworms and whipworms require a microscope to detect them. Diarrhea and vomiting, along with hair and weight loss, are evidence that your dog is suffering from a worm infestation.

A completely different internal parasite, and the most deadly, is the heartworm. Known in the United States for over a century, heartworm has been reported in all fifty states, though the main concentration of cases occurs along the Northeast and South. Heartworm is transmitted to dogs through mosquitoes that bite infected dogs. It takes six months for the larvae to mature into an adult worm.

Heartworm in dogs is fairly treatable, but it is extremely preventable. The American Heartworm Society recommends that all dog owners discuss heartworm-prevention options with their vets. Options include monthly or daily oral medication, a monthly topical, or a six-month shot.

SPAYING AND NEUTERING

The American Kennel Club recommends that all owners spay and neuter their pet dogs as a responsible measure to prevent unintentional matings and unwanted litters. The AKC encourages breeders to discuss spaying and neutering for all puppy

The Mighty Mites

Fleas and ticks aren't the only external parasites your dog can encounter. A *Demodex* mite infestation (or mange) commonly affects puppies, though adult dogs with compromised immune systems can develop cases. Ear mites, most commonly *Otodectes cynotis*, are highly contagious and are typically passed to dogs by feline companions. If your dog is scratching at his ears, holding his head to one side, shaking his head, producing a dark-colored wax, ear mites are the likely cause. Your vet can prescribe a treatment to eradicate both ear mites and *Demodex* mites.

Other Vaccines and Treatment

Depending on where you live and your dog's needs, the following ailments and diseases can be treated through your veterinarian:

CONDITION	TREATMENT	PROGNOSIS	RECOMMENDATION
BORDETELLA (KENNEL COUGH)	Keep warm; humidify room; moderate exercise	Highly contagious; rarely fatal in healthy dogs; easily treated	Optional vaccine; prevalence varies; vaccine may be linked to acute reactions; low efficacy
FLEA AND TICK INFESTATION	Topical and ingestible medications	Highly contagious	Preventive treatment highly recommended
HEARTWORM	Arsenical compound; rest; restricted exercise	Widely occurring infections; preventive programs available regionally; successful treatment after early detection	Preventive treatment highly recommended; treating an infected dog has some risks
INTESTINAL WORMS	Dewormer; home medication regimen	Good with prompt treatment	Preventive treatment highly recommended
LYME DISEASE (BORRELIOSIS)	Antibiotics	Can't completely eliminate the organism, but can be controlled in most cases	Vaccine recommended only for dogs with high risk of exposure to deer ticks
PARAINFLUENZA	Rest; humidify room; moderate exercise	Highly contagious; mild; self-limiting; rarely fatal	Vaccine optional but recommended; doesn't block infection, but lessens clinical signs
PERIODONTITIS	Dental cleaning; extractions; repair	Excellent, but involves anesthesia	Preventive treatment recommended

A PIECE OF HISTORY

Essentially the breed's modern history begins in 1905 when Richard Strebel's book *Die Deutschen Hunde und Ihre Abstammung* (German Dogs and Their Descent) was published and included the first detailed reference to the Rottweiler breed, though the drawing of the breed in the book was lankier and lighter in bone than today's Rottweiler.

This same year the Dog Show of the Association of the Friends of Dogs in Heidelberg was staged, and Albert Graf began promoting an unusual breed called the Rottweiler. Within a year, Graf was showing his Rottweiler Russ vom Brückenbuckel who won three international shows in 1906. Graf, along with Karl Knauf, established the Deutscher Rottweiler-Klub (DRK), and Russ was the first dog registered and would become the breed's most prolific sire in the early years, accounting for eighty dogs in the first DRK stud book (1907-1914).

buyers who are not planning to participate in conformation dog shows. Technically, spaying is the surgical removal of a female dog's uterus and ovaries, and neutering is the surgical removal of the male's testicles and spermatic cords. Do not spay or neuter your Rottweiler too early. Consult your veterinarian for advice about the appropriate age.

The only activity in which spayed and neutered dogs cannot participate is conformation. The American Kennel Club welcomes all dogs to participate in obedience, agility, tracking, herding, and other events. Check out the next chapter for more details about these fun events.

Playing in a nearby stream with a herding-dog chum is a great way to cool off on a warm day. A quick bath when these two get home would be well advised.

At a Glance ...

Know your Rottweiler's signs of wellness so that you recognize when he's not acting and feeling like his usual self.

. . . .

Exercise will keep your dog (and you) fit and healthy! Don't engage your puppy in strenuous activities until he's grown into his frame.

. . . .

When it comes to selecting a veterinarian, you want a caring, knowledgeable professional who stays current on veterinary advances, communicates clearly, and offers a variety of services. Consider location and cost as well.

. . . .

Be sure to keep your Rottweiler up to date on all core vaccinations and find out which other ones are recommended and how often.

. . . .

Do everything you can to prevent parasites, both external and internal. Fleas, ticks, and worms can be very harmful to your dog's health as well as your own.

. . . .

Discuss spaying or neutering your pet Rottweiler with your veterinarian.

CHAPTER ELEVEN

Rotties Do It All!

Rottweiler people know that there's no breed as remarkable and versatile as their beloved black and tans! If you're a member of this proud group, then the best thing you can do for your dog and the Rottweiler breed is to get out there and show the world what makes this breed so exceptional. Just by walking your well-heeled Rottie through the neighborhood or visiting a dog park, you're demonstrating to everyone how reliable and obedient the Rottweiler can be. But Rotties can do more than behave in public, they in fact can do it all!

Are you ready to explore the countless ways your Rottweiler can strut his stuff? Dog shows, obedience and agility trials, tracking tests, herding trials, therapy work...the list goes on and so do the Rottie's talents.

SHOWING

Today dog shows are popular around the world, not just in the United States and Europe, and the Rottweiler is an international favorite. Unlike Cocker Spaniels and Poodles, who have much more coat, the Rottweiler is a true "wash and wear" show dog, requiring nothing more than a bath and a brushing to turn the judge's head.

The American Kennel Club sponsors about 4,000 all-breed dog shows a year. There are two basic types of shows: all-breed shows, where most (if not all) AKC-recognized breeds can compete, and specialty shows, where one breed or one group competes. The American Rottweiler Club holds an annual national specialty, and each regional breed club holds its own specialty. Hundreds of Rotties and their owners participate in these shows, which can offer both conformation classes and agility trials as well as the German-style Sieger shows.

The AKC refers to dog shows as conformation shows because judges evaluate the dogs entered in their rings by how well they conform to the breed standard.

Shaka at Westminster and Beyond

The Rottweiler has been competing at the famed Westminster Kennel Club dog show since 1935, and it took until the 1980s for the breed to place in the Group Finally, in 2006, a Rottweiler took the honors of first in the Working Group. The dog named Ch. Carter's Noble Shaka Zulu, owned and handled by Keith Carter. Bred by Keith Carter and Nancy Noble, "Shaka" won more all-breed Bests in Shows than any other Rottie—a total of 39. He also won the ARC National three times and in 2005 won the Best Bred-by Exhibitor in Show at the AKC/Eukanuba National.

The Rottweiler who most closely resembles the ideal specimen as described in the standard is selected as Best of Breed. At all-breed shows, all of the Best of Breed winners proceed to compete in their respective groups with a new judge. The Rottweiler, therefore, competes against all of the other Working Group Best of Breed winners to determine the best in the group, or Group One. Once the seven groups have been judged, a new judge determines which of the seven group winners is Best in Show and Reserve Best in Show.

A dog becomes an AKC Champion by winning 15 points at AKC dog shows with two "major" wins (3 points or higher) under three different judges. The dog earns points by defeating other dogs of the same sex and breed in classes held for

Many well-trained Rottweilers excel as military and police dogs. These dogs are employed by the West Midlands Police Department.

Athletic and highly trainable, Rottweilers are frequently seen acing their courses at obedience and agility trials. This Rottie is practicing his jumping skills.

nonchampion dogs. Only one male and one female dog can earn championship points at a show, which means the dog has to be named Winners Dog or Winners Bitch (the awards for the best nonchampion dogs at the show).

OBEDIENCE TRIALS

Compared to conformation shows that go back to the late nineteenth century, obedience trials are a more recent development, though by no means a new sport. The American Kennel Club began hosting obedience trials in 1936, and today there are about 2,500 obedience trials held annually, most held in conjunction with dog

What's a Sieger Show?

German-style dog show vary significantly from American shows, and many Rottweiler clubs offer Sieger shows at their specialties. The handlers are not allowed to use food bait or stack their dogs in the ring, but instead a second handler uses a toy to bait the dog. Judges seek a Rottweiler who exhibits confidence and a strong prey drive. The dogs are also run around the ring for the judge to evaluate their movement and fitness. The judges' oral critiques of each dog in the ring are broadcasted over a sound system and printed critiques are available after the show.

Favor, the Favorite

The first Rottweiler to earn the elusive OTCH title (Obedience Trail Champion) was OTCH Mondberg's Donnamira V Beier, owned and trained by George L. Beck. Her call name was "Favor" and she died in December 1976.

shows. The exercises in obedience trials haven't changed all that much since the early days, though the rules have become more demanding over the years. The historic first obedience trial included: heel on leash and off leash; two-minute sit (with handler out of sight); recall; retrieving a dumbbell and jumping over obstacle with it; six-foot long jump; and a five-minute down. A modern Rottie who could ace all of those exercises would still be taking home ribbons today.

The first title a dog can earn at an obedience trial is the Companion Dog (CD), which requires heeling on and off leash, coming when called, standing still while the judge touches the dog, and staying in both the sitting and lying down positions until released by the handler. The Companion Dog Excellent (CDX) includes off-leash heeling, longer stays, retrieving and jumping. Tests for Utility Dog (UD), the next level, are all off leash and include directed retrieving, where the handler signals the dog to pick up three selected objects; scent discrimination, where the dog must choose one of several objects touched by the handler; and extended stays. Once a dog earns one of these titles, a suffix (the initials of the title) is placed after his name. The highest AKC obedience title is the prefix, Obedience Trial Champion (OTCH), for dogs who have earned a UD and received a required number of first places in continued competition.

AGILITY

A relatively new AKC sport, agility began 1994 and, in just two short decades, has hurdled far ahead of obedience in popularity. Today agility is the fastest growing AKC sport. An agility trial is essentially a timed obstacle course for dogs and handlers. The sport requires the dog to maneuver over several obstacles as led by the handler, who runs along with the dog. The winning dog is the one who completes the course the fastest with the highest score (losing the fewest points for technical mistakes). The obstacles include jumps of various heights and shapes, teeter-totters, balance beams, tunnels, and poles. Any dog who takes obstacles without the handler's direction, knocks a jump down, or fails to touch his paws in designated places loses points. Positive training is the key to mastering agility, and active, energetic dogs enjoy the challenge and excitement of these fast-paced trials. The best way to get your Rottie started with agility trials is to join a training club in your area. Agility training groups have all of the equipment required at a trial as well as experienced handlers to show you and your dog the ropes. Dogs must be at least one year of age to participate in an AKC agility trial.

Did You Know?

The Rottweiler can do it all, or so it seems as many owners like to capitalize on the breed's astonishing versatility. Not only does the breed excel as a herding dog and a police dog, it also has been used as a search and rescue dog and a tracking dog. The breed's excellent nose and soft mouth have also found it acclaim as a hunting dog. Some owners report that they have worked game birds, such as ducks and pheasants, as well as rabbit and hare in open fields with their Rotties. Once a Rottweiler is trained, there's little he can't do once he puts his mind to it.

Scaling the heights (and the jumps) come naturally to the athletic Rottweiler.

Radar on Course!

The first Rottweiler to earn the MACH title, the highest title in agility, was OTCH MACH2 Esp Aces Levi's Topgun Radar UDX4 MXB2 MJB2, trained and owned by his breeder Elaine Swancer. According to AKC records, Radar was the first Rottweiler to achieve Master Brown, Silver, Gold, and Century Jumper and Agility titles, as well as the Master Bronze Jumper 2 title: that's ten firsts in agility!

RALLY

AKC rally is a fun transitional sport that takes dogs and owners from the AKC Canine Good Citizen test to agility trials. This sport is fast-paced like agility and requires a degree of precision like obedience. Any Rottie, six months of age and older, who is registered (or listed) with the AKC is eligible to compete. At their own pace, handlers and their dogs enter a course marked by ten to twenty signs, designed by the judge. Each sign gives a direction such as "Send Over Jump," "Slow Forward From Sit," and "Double Left About Turn." The handler can talk to his dog as much as necessary, though he cannot touch him. Unlike obedience, the dog does not have to heel perfectly as he follows his handler around the course. Rally is geared toward both pet owners and fanciers, and its main goal is to promote teamwork between owner and dog. Outside the ring in their everyday lives, CGC and rally dogs are model citizens who can be mannerly at home, in public places, and with other dogs.

TRACKING

Tracking is the nose sport for dogs, the competitive version of canine search and rescue. The fundamental features of a Tracking Dog (TD) test are the dog's ability to follow a track laid by a person under a variety of conditions on moderate terrain and to find an article dropped by that person at the end of the track. Tracking events provide a basis for training to meet real-life tasks, such as finding a lost person or detecting specific substances for border-control or airport work, e.g., illegal drugs, accelerants, insects, fruit, and so forth.

In order to participate, a dog must be six months of age and pass a certification test signed by an approved tracking judge. At a tracking event, the dog is in a harness with a long leash that the handler holds but cannot use to direct the dog. To begin, the handler lets the dog sniff an object with the tracklayer's scent, indicates to the dog where the track starts, and then follows along behind the dog as he follows the track. The dog is required to keep working at the track and not get distracted by wildlife, other dogs, etc. If the dog strays from the course and does not return to it, the test ends. AKC offers five tracking titles, each varying in difficulty and requirements: Tracking Dog (TD), Tracking Dog Excellent (TDX), Variable Surface Tracking (VST), Tracking Dog Urban (TDU), and Champion Tracker (CT).

HERDING EVENTS

The Rottweiler's origin as a drover dog has earned him entry into AKC herding events. Owners interested in herding trials must begin training prior to entering a trial by exposing their dogs to livestock. AKC offers two types of herding events, noncompetitive and competitive. A noncompetitive herding test offers owners a way to gauge their dogs' basic herding instincts and trainability. Competitive herding trials aim to preserve and expand a dog's inherent skills to demonstrate that he can do the work for which his breed was developed. Based on simulations of farm work, herding trials are standardized to measure and develop specific breed characteristics.

An instinct test is the first test a herding dog can take, and the dog need not be trained prior to entering the class. This initial test allows a judge to assess a dog's innate ability to fetch and drive livestock. AKC offers over a dozen herding titles, from Herding Tested (HT) all the way through Herding Champion (HC).

Although the Rottweiler isn't a full-fledged member of the Herding Group, the breed participates alongside the Belgian Malinois and other Herding breeds at herding events.

THERAPY WORK

There can be no better ambassador for the breed than a charismatic, well-trained Rottweiler working as a therapy dog in nursing homes, retirement facilities, and hospitals. The basic requirement of a therapy dog is a reliable temperament, a people-loving disposition, and basic obedience. The steady disposition, solid construction, and physical size of the Rottie give him the advantage of not being bothered by the clattering of a walker or an inadvertent bump from wheelchair. The Rottie is a good sport with a lovable sense of humor and a natural affinity for attention.

A Rottweiler cannot be a great therapy dog without his owner and handler fully committing to the activity, which many people regard as more of a ministry than a hobby. Before your Rottie can begin brightening the faces and lives of patients, he will need to be tested and certified.

The AKC Canine Good Citizen test is the gold standard of therapy dogs, and most therapy-dog registries require that dogs pass the CGC test. The AKC Therapy Dog program awards the "ThD" title to any registered therapy dog who has performed a certain number of visits per year. AKC works with over fifty-five organizations that register therapy dogs, including Bright and Beautiful Therapy Dogs, Pet Partners (formerly the Delta Society), Therapy Dogs Inc., and Therapy Dogs International. Each registry has different criteria for being registered. For more information, visit www.akc.org/akctherapydog.

Discover your Rottweiler's passion. This Rottie is playing flyball on a sunny beach with his fun-loving owner.

Rottweiler ACEs

In 2000, the AKC instituted the AKC Humane Fund Awards for Canine Excellence to honor dogs who excel in certain areas of canine service. Each year one dog is honored in one of five categories: law enforcement, search and rescue, therapy, service, and exemplary companion dog.

FAITH

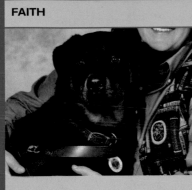

In 2005, the AKC awarded the ACE Award for a Service Dog to "Faith," a four-year-old Rottweiler who saved her owner Leana Beasley's life on September 7, 2004 when she collapsed from a grand mal seizure. After extensive training in seizure, cardiac, and respiratory alert from the Assistance Dog Club of Puget Sound, Faith was able to dial 9-1-1, bark into the receiver, roll her owner into recovery position, and unlock a door to allow police in to rescue her owner who was in extreme distress.

RUMOR

The 2007 ACE Exemplary Companion Dog award went to "Rumor," a four-year-old Rottweiler owned by Francisco Sanguino and Steph Anderson. Both Francisco, a teenager, and Rumor, a rescue dog, came to foster parent Steph Anderson from difficult situations. Rumor was Francisco's first experience with unconditional love, and through the spirit and generosity of this dog, Francisco began to flourish in his new home, setting goals for himself, and being hopeful about his future. Together this accomplished pair became involved in Junior Showmanship, rally, obedience, and therapy work.

BENNY

The 2012 ACE Therapy Dog Award went to nine-year-old "Benny," owned by Kelly Skiptunas, who logged in more than 250 hours of therapy-dog visits at a local hospital, a rehabilitation center, and an assisted-living facility. Benny was a show dog in the United States and Canada and holds the AKC Therapy Dog title and the AKC CGC title. Benny appeared on public TV as do-good ambassador for the breed and is certified as a "READ" dog (Reading Education Assistance Dog) who visits libraries to be read stories by young students.

WORKING AND VERSATILE SCHUTZHUND DOGS

AKC recognizes Working Dog titles awarded by the DVG (Deutscher Verband der Gebrauchshundsportvereine), the German organization that is dedicated to Schutzhund training. Founded in 1903 as Germany's first police dog and service dog club, the DVG today consists of over 30,000 members and holds about 1,900 trials a year. Visit www.dvgamerica.com for more information.

There is an American "region" (or Landesverband, in German) for the DVG called the LV/DVG America. The titles awarded by the DVG are acceptable to add to a dog's AKC name.

The VDH Working Dog Council (AZG) recently decided to rename the sport to reflect the versatility that has always been at the heart of Schutzhund. The new name is abbreviated VPG, which stands for Vielseitigkeitspruefung fuer Gebrauchshunde, or Versatility Test for Working Dogs. Versatile Schutzhund dog sport (hundesport) focuses on training, tracking, obedience, and protection or bitework. Most people familiar with Schutzhund usually associate it specifically with protection training, although that is only one of the three phases of testing.

Titles from the Fatherland

TITLE	GERMAN TERM	PURPOSE	MINIMUM AGE
BH	Begleithundprüfung	Temperament title	15 months
IPO1, IPO2, IPO3	Internationale Prufungsordnung	Schutzhund titles (FCI)	18, 19, 20 months
SchHa & SchH1	Schutzhund	Versatility tests	18 months
SchH 2	Schutzhund	Versatility test	19 months
SchH 3	Schutzhund	Versatility test	20 months
FH1	Fahrtenhund	Tracking test	16 months
FH2	Fahrtenhund	Tracking test	20 months

- Tracking Phase, similar to AKC tracking, including following a person over various terrains and locating lost articles
- Obedience Phase, similar to AKC trials but set on a large open field, including on- and off-lead heeling, sit, down, stand, recall, send out, and retrieving dumbbell over a jump and six-foot wall
- Protection Phase, controlled attack work in which dog must attack without hesitation and then stop biting upon the handler's command

REGIONAL ROTTWEILER CLUBS

Rottweiler fanciers are fortunate to have over twenty AKC regional clubs dedicated to the breed in the United States, including clubs in all four regions of the country as well as Alaska and Hawaii. California, Florida, Arizona, and Ohio each have two regional clubs: Associated Fanciers of Northern California and the Southwestern Rottweiler Club of San Diego in California; Gulf Stream Rottweiler Club of Greater Miami and Seminole Rottweiler Club of North Central Florida in the Sunshine State; Golden State Rottweiler Club and Grand Canyon State Rottweiler Club in Arizona; and Emerald Valley Rottweiler Club of Great Cleveland and Greater Cincinnati Rottweiler Club in Ohio.

Owners of sunbathing Rotties in Hawaii can join the Aloha State Rottweiler Club, and those snow-loving Rotties in The Last Frontier state can belong to the Rottweiler Club of Alaska.

Rottweiler Clubs

Visit the ARC website to find a list of regional breed clubs, organized by state. Breed clubs are an excellent way to connect with other Rottweiler owners and lovers. Clubs offer training classes and seminars for various disciplines and keep members informed about important Rottweiler-related events and issues.

Some Rottweilers can't be convinced that they can't do it all. This athletic Rottie is competing in dock diving.

In the South there are the Colonial Rottweiler Club in Virginia, Dogwood Rottweiler Club of Metropolitan Atlanta in Georgia, and the Texican Rottweiler Club in Texas. In the Midwest we have Badger State Rottweiler Fanciers (Wisconsin); Medallion Rottweiler Club (Illinois); Hoosier Rottweiler Club (Indiana); Great Lakes Rottweiler Club of Southeast Michigan (Michigan), and Northstar Rottweiler Club (Minnesota).

The great state of New York has the Greater New York Rottweiler Club. In Oregon, there's Columbia River Rottweiler Club; in Colorado, Mile-High Rottweiler Club of Greater Denver; and for those desert dwellers in the Land of Enchantment, the Rottweiler Club of New Mexico.

At a Glance ...

Dog shows, or conformation shows, are the American Kennel Club's signature event, and Rottweilers love to strut their stuff in front of the judge and the crowds.

. . . .

Rottweilers successfully compete in a variety of AKC trials including obedience, rally, agility, and tracking. Because of their cattle-dog background, Rotties can also compete in herding events.

. . . .

Do your part to preach the gospel of the Rottweiler: register your dog as a therapy dog, become an AKC Canine Good Citizen, and show the community how wonderful real Rotties are!

. . . .

Americans have embraced many of the tests and trials from the Rottweiler's Fatherland. Working Dog events test the dog's training in the disciplines of tracking, obedience, and protection work.

Resources

BOOKS

The American Kennel Club's Meet the Breeds: Dog Breeds from A to Z, 4th edition (Irvine, California: i5 Press, 2014) The ideal puppy buyer's guide, this book has all you need to know about each breed currently recognized by the AKC.

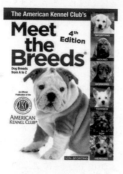

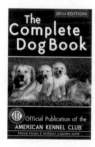

The Complete Dog Book, 20th edition (New York: Ballantine Books, 2006) This official publication of the AKC, first published in 1929, includes the complete histories and breed standards of 153 recognized breeds, as well as information on general care and the dog sport.

The Complete Dog Book for Kids (New York: Howell Book House, 1996) Specifically geared toward young people, this official publication of the AKC presents 149 breeds and varieties, as well as introductory owners' information.

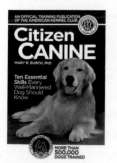

Citizen Canine: Ten Essential Skills Every Well-Mannered Dog Should Know by Mary R. Burch, PhD (Irvine, California: i5 Press, 2010) This official AKC publication is the definitive guide to the AKC's Canine Good Citizen® Program, recognized as the gold standard of behavior for dogs, with more than half a million dogs trained.

DOGS: The First 125 Years of the American Kennel Club (Irvine, California: i5 Press, 2009) This official AKC publication presents an authoritative, complete history of the AKC, including detailed information not found in any other volume.

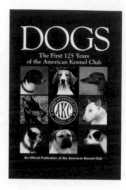

Dog Heroes of September 11th: A Tribute to America's Search and Rescue Dogs, 10th anniversary edition, by Nona Kilgore Bauer (Irvine, California: i5 Press, 2011) A publication to salute the canines that served in the recovery missions following the September 11th attacks, this book serves as a lasting tribute to these noble American heroes.

The Original Dog Bible: The Definitive Source for All Things Dog, 2nd edition, by Kristin Mehus-Roe (Irvine, California: i5 Press, 2009) This 831-page magnum opus includes more than 250 breed profiles, hundreds of color photographs, and a wealth of information on every dog topic imaginable—thousands of practical tips on grooming, training, care, and much more.

PERIODICALS

American Kennel Club Gazette

Every month since 1889, serious dog fanciers have looked to the *AKC Gazette* for authoritative advice on training, showing, breeding, and canine health. Each issue includes the breed columns section, written by experts from the respective breed clubs. Only available electronically.

AKC Family Dog

This is a bimonthly magazine for the dog lover whose special dog is "just a pet." Helpful tips, how-tos, and features are written in an entertaining and reader-friendly format. It's a lifestyle magazine for today's busy families who want to enjoy a rewarding, mutually happy relationship with their canine companions.

Dog Fancy

The world's most widely read dog magazine, *Dog Fancy* celebrates dogs and the people who love them. Each monthly issue includes info on cutting-edge medical developments, health and fitness (with a focus on prevention,

treatment, and natural therapy), behavior and training, travel and activities, breed profiles and dog news, issues and trends for dog owners. The magazine informs, inspires, and entertains while promoting responsible dog ownership. Throughout its more than forty-year history, *Dog Fancy* has garnered numerous honors, including being named the Best All-Breed Magazine by the Dog Writers Association of America.

Dogs in Review

For more than fifteen years, *Dogs in Review* has showcased the finest dogs in the United States and from around the world. The emphasis has always been on strong content, with input from distinguished breeders, judges, and handlers worldwide. This global perspective distinguishes this monthly publication from its competitors—no other North American dog-show magazine gathers together so many international experts to enlighten and entertain its readership.

Dog World

Dog World is an annual lifestyle magazine published by the editors of *Dog Fancy* that covers all aspects of the dog world: culture, art, history, travel, sports, and science. It also profiles breeds to help prospective owners choose the best dogs for their future needs, such as a potential show champion, super service dog, great pet, or competitive star.

Natural Dog

Natural Dog is the magazine dedicated to giving a dog a natural lifestyle. From nutritional choices to grooming to dog-supply options, this publication helps readers make the transition from traditional to natural methods. The magazine also explores the array of complementary treatments available for today's dogs: acupuncture, massage, homeopathy, aromatherapy,

and much more. *Natural Dog* appears as an annual publication and also as the flip side of *Dog Fancy* magazine occasionally.

Puppies USA

Also from the editors of *Dog Fancy*, this annual magazine offers essential information for all new puppy owners. *Puppies USA* is lively and informative, including advice on general care, nutrition, grooming, and training techniques for all puppies, whether purebred or mixed breed, adopted, rescued, or purchased. In addition, it offers family fun through quizzes, contests, and much more. An extensive breeder directory is included.

WEBSITES

www.akc.org

The American Kennel Club (AKC) website is an excellent starting point for researching dog breeds and learning about puppy care. The site lists hundreds of breeders, along with basic information about breed selection and basic care. The site also has links to the national breed club of every AKC-recognized breed; breed-club sites offer plenty of detailed breed information, as well as lists of member breeders. In addition, you can find the AKC National Breed Club Rescue List at www.akc.org/breeds/rescue.cfm. If looking for purebred puppies, go to www.puppybuyerinfo.com for AKC classifieds and parent-club referrals.

www.dogchannel.com

Powered by *Dog Fancy*, Dog Channel is "the website for dog lovers," where hundreds of thousands of visitors each month find extensive information on breeds, training, health and nutrition, puppies, care, activities, and more. Interactive features include forums, Dog College, games, and Club Dog, a free club where dog lovers can create blogs for their pets and earn points to buy products. Dog Channel is the one-stop site for all things dog.

www.meetthebreeds.com

The official website of the AKC Meet the Breeds® event, hosted by the American Kennel Club in New York City. The first Meet the Breeds event took place in 2009. AKC Meet the Breeds offers pet lovers a unique opportunity to get up close and personal with some of the country's rarest dog breeds. Spectators can talk to responsible breeders and owners about these amazing animals and determine the right breed for their lifestyle.

AKC AFFILIATES

The **AKC Museum of the Dog**, established in 1981, is located in St. Louis, Missouri, and houses the world's finest collection of art devoted to the dog. Visit www.museumofthedog.org.

The **AKC Humane Fund** promotes the joy and value of responsible and productive pet ownership through education, outreach, and grant-making. Monies raised may fund grants to organizations that teach responsible pet ownership; provide for the health and well-being of all dogs; and preserve and celebrate the human-animal bond and the evolutionary relationship between dogs and humankind. Go to www.akchumanefund.org.

AKC Reunite is dedicated to reuniting lost microchipped and tattooed pets with their owners. AKC Reunite maintains a permanent-identification database and provides lifetime recovery services 24 hours a day, 365 days a year, for all animal species. Millions of pets are enrolled in the program, which was established in 1995. Visit www.akcreunite.org.

The **American Kennel Club Canine Health Foundation (AKC CHF), Inc.** is the largest foundation in the world to fund canine-only health studies for purebred and mixed-breed dogs. More than $22 million has been allocated in research funds to more than 500 health studies conducted to help dogs live longer, healthier lives. Go to www.akcchf.org.

AKC PROGRAMS

The **Canine Good Citizen Program (CGC)** was established in 1989 and is designed to recognize dogs that have good manners at home and in the community. This rapidly growing, nationally recognized program stresses responsible dog ownership for owners and basic training and good manners for dogs. All dogs that pass the ten-step Canine Good Citizen test receive a certificate from the American Kennel Club. Go to www.akc.org/events/cgc.

The **AKC S.T.A.R. Puppy Program** is designed to get dog owners and their puppies off to a good start and is aimed at loving dog owners who have taken the time to attend basic obedience classes with their puppies. After completing a six-week training course, the puppy must pass the AKC S.T.A.R. Puppy test, which evaluates Socialization, Training, Activity, and Responsibility. Go to www.akc.org/starpuppy.

The **AKC Therapy Dog** program recognizes all American Kennel Club dogs and their owners who have given their time and helped people by volunteering as a therapy dog-and-owner team. The AKC Therapy Dog program is an official American Kennel Club title awarded to dogs that have worked to improve the lives of the people they have visited. The AKC Therapy Dog title (AKC ThD) can be earned by dogs that have been certified by recognized therapy dog organizations. For more information, visit www.akc.org/akctherapydog.

Index

AMERICAN KENNEL CLUB®

Advocating for the purebred dog as a family companion, advancing canine health and well-being, working to protect the rights of all dog owners, and promoting responsible dog ownership, the **American Kennel Club:**

Sponsors more than **22,000 sanctioned events** annually, including conformation, agility, obedience, rally, tracking, lure coursing, earthdog, herding, field trial, hunt test, and coonhound events.

Features a **ten-step Canine Good Citizen® program** that rewards dogs who have good manners at home and in the community

Has reunited more than **400,000** lost pets with their owners through AKC Reunite—visit **www.akcreunite.org**

Created and supports the AKC Canine Health Foundation, which funds research projects using the more than **$22 million** the AKC has donated since 1995—visit **www.akcchf.org**

Joins **animal lovers** through education, outreach, and grant-making via the AKC Humane Fund—visit **www.akchumanefund.org**

We're more than champion dogs. We're the dog's champion.

www.akc.org